Tractor Bones and Rusted Trucks; Tales and Recollections of a Heartland Baby Boomer

By

Greg Seeley

Printed in the United States of America

First Printing, 2018

ISBN 978-1719-575-409

ISBN 1-719-575-401

Edited by Katie-bree Reeves of
Fair Crack of the Whip Proofreading and Editing

Cover design by Paul Copello of Designistrate.com

Other Books by Greg Seeley

The Horse Lawyer and Other Poems (2014)
Henry's Pride (2016)
Henry's Land (Fall 2018)

ACKNOWLEDGMENTS

A special thank you to all of the friends, relatives, and colleagues who have contributed their time and support to this project.

Thank you to my editor, Katie-bree Reeves who brought rare talent, along with her understanding and passion for farm life, to his endeavor.

To my cover designer, Paul Copello, for his care and professionalism in creating a design that captures the real essence of my poems and stories.

Most of all, thank you to my wife Carolyn - for your love, support, patience, and understanding as I work to present this picture of the middle America that we both remember as children and teens.

DEDICATION

This collection of poems and essays is dedicated to Carolyn, my beautiful wife of 49 years – the love of my life, who grew up driving tractors, feeding chickens, and pulling button weeds from the family soybean fields. To this remarkable woman who has patiently put up with all (or most) of my quirks, oddities, and eccentricities for her entire adult life, **Thank you!**

CONTENTS

PART II -STORIES FROM MINLEY

PREFACE

We are expatriates now, many of us – the farm kids of the late forties, the fifties and the sixties. We are removed by time, distance, and either fortune or choice from the farms where we spent our growing-up years. Our parents and our neighbors, from whom we learned their values and ways, had been mostly children of the Great Depression. They were children in a time when saving and "making do" were everything and "work" and "survival" were synonymous. If the farm was paid for, or if there was enough money from selling crops or livestock to pay the rent or the mortgage, there was food and shelter. Clothes were mostly made at home from whatever material was available. Once outgrown, they were patched up and handed down to the next brother or sister. All else, if there *was* anything else, was extra. Most had few extras.

The children of the Depression grew into the young adults of wartime. Many young farmers, some by their own wishes – others not - were exempt from the draft. Soldiers, sailors, marines, and airmen needed food and America needed farmers to provide it. Most farmers, in turn, were yet to have their first tractor. The war meant jobs. Jobs meant money. But there wasn't much to buy. Sugar and flour were rationed. So were tires, gasoline, and nearly everything else. As before, homemade became the rule. Butter came from the cow, the cream separator, and a churn. Eggs were gathered from the henhouse. Meat came from the barnyard, not from the store. School clothes came from the sewing machine and the bags that had recently held chicken feed. The mantra was "Use it up. Wear it out. Make it do or do without!" It was all done without electricity. FDR's Rural Electrification Administration had promised electricity for the farms. As with many other things postponed by the war, that would have to wait.

It was these times and these trials that shaped our parents and reinforced in them a culture of hard work, faith, frugality, strength in the face of adversity, and a sense of community. It was these parents, molded by their own experiences, who created and raised us – the farm kids of the 50's and 60's.

We grew into a world where the tractors, pickup trucks, and combines that had replaced the draft horses, wooden wagons, and threshing machines were themselves beginning to give out – repaired as far as possible during the war and now reaching their end. Worn out and of little trade-in value, many were towed to the corners of pastures and left to be overgrown with weeds and saplings. It was the age of *Tractor Bones and Rusted Trucks*.

Poems from the Farm

Tractor Bones and Rusted Trucks

I found a cemetery, when I was young,
In the corner of a neighbor's field
Where his land met ours.
It wasn't neat and wasn't kept.
The grass was tall and the weeds were taller.
No one came to mourn or bring flowers.
The only bouquets were native-grown.

Only the bones of tractors here,
Machines of other sorts,
And ancient pickup trucks -
Brought to rest
When time and use had taken their toll
And the mechanics could do no more
To make them run
Or even of use for trade.

There were no stones or markers -
None were needed.
Paint and names no longer visible,
I knew them all by name;
John Deere, McCormick, Ford,
And Dodge and J.I. Case.
The green and yellow were long-since gone,
As were the red and black.
The equalizer had begun his work
And coated each
With notations of his own
In reddish brown.

The Dodge behind the Chicken House

Grandpa bought his pickup new
In 1932 and wore it out before the war.
He'd planned to replace it
In the spring of 1942
But there were none
To be had by then.

"Make it do," the new mantra said
And so, he did.
Scoured salvage yards
When parts were needed,
Wired others back in place,
And drove the tires bald.

He parked it behind the chicken house
When the war was over –
Had no trade-in value for his new one
And the War Department
Was no longer buying scrap.

My cousin and I
Found it in the weeds
And made it ours.
It was our big adventure
For most of one summer.
We drove it over the road
In our young imaginations
And made it fly over wartime skies.
We packed at least a dozen lunches
For long-haul trips
And flights over enemy lands.
But we left it alone forever
When a swarm of bees
Took up residence under the seat.

The Behemoth Beyond the Hay Yard

I am the iron behemoth
That sleeps in the grove of Poplar trees
In the corner of the pasture
Just beyond the hay yard.

I wait to awaken and face my fate,
To be hauled away and melted down –
Reincarnated perhaps
Into a newer version of myself –
Or restored perhaps
To the glory of my younger days –
Painted fresh, my gears repaired and oiled
And brought out for parades and shows –
Or left perhaps
To remain among the trees
To decay
And become one
With the land that I once ruled.

I remember how the ground once trembled
As I rolled across
And churned it
With the force of my wheels,
Pulling with the power
Of a dozen or more horses
A great 12-bottom plow.

I remember the unquenchable thirst
In my boiler
For all the water
They could bring me from the well
To where I powered
The shaking, rattling, noisy, threshing machine.

I remember the insatiable hunger
In my great belly
For all of the coal they would bring
To keep my pulley turning
To saw their firewood and lumber.

I boasted once, proudly and loudly,
Of my power
To all who could hear my fiery belch
Of smoke and steam.

I am the iron behemoth
That sleeps among the trees and waits.

Peddlers

We didn't call them peddlers.
No wagons drawn by horses,
Rattling with pots and pans,
Or other kitchen goods

They arrived in cars
Or new vehicles called station wagons
Filled with the latest gadgets -
Free samples of spices, extracts,
And other wonders
And as much product
As they could sell.
They were the ...... man.
Fuller Brush, Watkins, and others
Whose names I can't recall.

There were brushes for cleaning dishes
And brushes for scrubbing potatoes
And cleaning the kitchen sink -
Expertly demonstrated
Just like the gadget guy
On stage at the state fair.

They came in pickups too,
With samples of steel gates.
There were loading chutes
And vaccinating chutes
And chicken feeders,
Hog feeders, and free pails
That proudly showed their name.
There was even feed –
Moorman, Walnut Grove.

It was fun to see them come
And listen to them talk
But nothing compared
To the Schwann's Ice-cream truck.

The Moses Bed

It was just a little grassy slough above the pond
That my sister named the Moses bed
For its tall grass and waterweeds
That reminded her of the bull rushes.

It wasn't a bed or a nest,
Though it was a bit marshy,
For a few days after a rain
Relieved the dust.

We never saw Moses
Or *any* Egyptian.
It didn't matter though,
To us.
It was shady from the willow and cottonwoods
And mostly cool on summer days
With lemonade
And some sandwiches made for the occasion.

Nothing much happened at the Moses bed
Except for dreams and play.

Others now might find the slough,
But never the Moses Bed.
It's our alone –forever hidden,
In the grass
Of a little slough above the pond.

The Summer of 1954

It was the summer of 1954.
I was six and many of them,
Were the age that I am now,
Who marched
In the little town's centennial parade.

They had fought in Europe's Great War,
The one that was supposed to be the last.
They followed a man in an open car
Who had ridden once
With Teddy Roosevelt in Cuba –
And were followed by much younger ones
Who'd fought again in Europe
And in the Pacific and Korea.

Behind came floats and flags and drums
And the high school marching band
And the local Boy Scout troop
With Cub Scouts trying to keep up.

There were wagons fixed up
And repainted for the occasion,
Now pulled by trucks or tractors,
That once had delivered coal and ice
And brought milk and eggs from local farms.
The mayor rode in an open buggy
Retrieved from a shed
Behind the Ford garage.

I was six.
I watched in wonder
As they passed the square
And headed toward the fairgrounds.
I watched and had no clue that it wouldn't last forever.

Fair Measure

The county fair,
Was just as fair of a measure
Of the failure or success
Of last year's crops
As the number of notices
For farm auctions or foreclosures
Posted in the window of the bank.

Bad harvest –
Few new tractors and corn pickers
Parked for show and sale
Outside of the exhibit hall,
"Can't afford inventory that we can't sell."
Good harvest -
New combines and balers
Pulled from their storage
In the FFA and 4-H barns
To make room for hogs and show calves.

Bad harvest –
Same old tractors
Participating in the tractor pull,
None of this year's model.
Good harvest –
New John Deeres and Farmalls,
Bigger, stronger,
Need more weight on the sled.

Bad harvest –
Same cars and trucks in the parking lot,
A year older, more miles,
More rust.
Good harvest –
This year's models, newest colors, more shine.

Bad harvest –
Lower attendance at the rodeo
And at the stock car races,
Frugal farmers spending less on entertainment.
Good harvest --
Overflowing crowds, more cotton candy,
More soda and burgers
Sold at the refreshment stand.

A One-lane Bridge

You can only find it now
With a snorkel or scuba gear
If it's even there at all,
And you know just where to look.

It was a one-lane steel truss bridge
That carried the narrow dirt road
Across Three Mile Creek,
That was over the hill,
Behind my best friend's house.

We'd go there once in a while
On summer afternoons
But I don't recall
That we ever swam or fished.
We'd climb up on it
Or hide out underneath
While an occasional car or tractor or pickup truck
Rumbled overhead.

We were adventurers and explorers –
Until the adventures became too small
And there was nothing left to explore
That we hadn't seen a dozen times.
We outgrew the little bridge
And discovered more grown-up pursuits
Like hay baling –
And girls.

Stockyards

Our town
Had a thriving stockyard once.
I only learned of it
From Grandpa.

Never heard the bellowing steers
Nor the squealing hogs
On the way to market.
Never heard the cursing handlers
Working recalcitrant livestock.
Never heard the belching locomotives
That hauled the animals to Omaha, St. Jo,
Or Kansas City
Before the age of semi-trailers.

I never saw the pens
That held stock driven to the yards
By farmers on foot or horseback
And never saw the loading chutes.
I found the remnants once
While exploring along the tracks
Just east of town –
Here and there a rotted post
Sticking stubbornly from the ground
Or a mushy piece of plank,
Moldy, grey, green
Once strong enough to support a steer.

Never heard it,
Never saw it,
Never smelled it –
But I close my eyes
And it's there again,

Granaries

They had names once,
And also pride,
Before time, the sun, the rain
And the wind and snow,
Made them anonymous
And retirement made them humble.

Wooden boxcars rode the rails once –
North, South, East, and West.
They were painted red
Or white or blue or orange
And carried grain, lumber, fruit,
And more than a few hoboes.

Frisco, Cotton Belt,
And *Everywhere West*
Decay behind the barns and cattle sheds,
On blocks instead of wheels,
Their bellies filled once a year at harvest
And emptied
Of their oats or hay by winter's end.

They sit –
Mocked by the noisy clack and rumble
From the nearby tracks.

Out to Pasture

They spent their days on an old park bench
Along the highway, in front of the filling station –
The same bench that their fathers had used before them,
Same spot, same road.

Old workhorses –
Retired from the barns and fields
Of their younger days –
Now freed from the harness of daily chores,
From plowing, from picking corn,
And from hauling straw and hay.

There was finally time to smoke their pipes,
To watch the traffic,
And to gripe about the same things
Their fathers had griped about before them,
"Too hot, too cold, too much rain, too little rain,
The politicians are messing up the country now.
Need Ike, need Truman, need FDR.
Folks were different in my day.
People used to show respect.
The younger generation
Is running itself into ruin."

Final Bell

They closed a couple at a time
Over several years.
Some too dilapidated
To be worth repairing.
Others moved
Becoming houses, town halls,
Or simply mindless, silent storage
For tools or grain.

And then, in 1958,
The county closed the rest.

"Not efficient," they said,
"To have a teacher with just twelve pupils
And teaching all eight grades –
Better to teach twenty-five
And teach the same thing
To all of them at once.
Can't have the youngsters learning
By listening to the older ones
Recite their lessons aloud."

"Not efficient," they said
"To have farm kids walk
Or ride their bikes to school and home
And eat the lunches their mothers sent.
Better to put forty on a bus
And haul them all to town
And serve the same lunch to all."

"Not safe," the county said
"To have big and little kids
Together on the playground.
Someone might fall down."

"Not safe to have them sledding
On the big hill just outside the school.
Leave the sleds at home.
And cut out paper snowflakes
When it's too cold to be outside."

We didn't have a voice as I recall –
Nor did our parents,
They told us later.
The county knew best
And sent us all to school in town.

On Tearing Down a Barn

I helped a neighbor
Tear down a barn
When I was young,
One whose time had come.

An empty barn should never suffer
A lingering demise –
Shouldn't be left
To fall of its own accord
When its timbered shoulders of oak or hickory
Can no longer hold the burden
Of ice and snow.

A barn should not be picked apart,
Piece by piece,
By the scavenger winds
That scour the countryside
Searching for an easy meal
Of shingles
Or loose-hinged doors and windows
Waiting to be carried away
And devoured.

An aged barn deserves
To be euthanized
Swiftly by a lightning bolt
From a sudden mid-summer storm
And leave the farm
In a majestic blaze
Worthy of a Viking warrior.

A weakened barn
Deserves to die
In the rapid fury of
Of a cyclonic storm
And die in moments,
Not in months or years.

And if nature waits too long
And needs a helping hand,
An ailing barn should still be taken down
With all the care
That was used to put it up.

Men of Steel

They were made of steel,
These men who walked behind their iron plows,
And later rode,
But breathed in mule or horse dust just the same.

They were made of steel,
And too, their sons,
Our dads, who rode on tractors
Across the fields
Through biting wind or searing heat
And ate the later generations
Of the same infernal, eternal dust.

They were harder on themselves
Than on the tools with which they worked –
And less forgiving of themselves
Than of their horses and machines
When illness, accident, or wearing out
Made them stop before the work was done.

Work paused to oil the gears
And make adjustments or repairs
Or rest the horse
Or bring a fresh one in
But not for muscle aches
Or calluses of their own
And rarely for a sprain.

Yet somehow most survived
And saw their horses or equipment sold
Or traded for new.
They continued on,
Though tired, worn,
And too soon old –

A Ford at the Creek

I searched the creek all summer
For the Ford that Grandpa said
Was there somewhere,
About a quarter-mile
Above the Three Mile Bridge.

I never discovered that old car
But never told him so –
Didn't want to disappoint him
That it wasn't there
Or admit I couldn't find it.
All I found was a shallow spot
That I could cross
And barely wet my feet.

Hidden Farms

Unlike in the churchyard,
There are no stones
To mark their place in history,
To show that they were ever there –
The only evidence of their existence
Fading, handwritten lines
On yellowing pages
In books on storage shelves
At the county recorder's office –
Cold and brief obituaries
That no one ever reads.

Here and there a foundation
Of a house or barn
Sits overgrown
At the end of a tree-lined lane
Or in the middle a field.
A spot is marked
But no one has bothered to write a name.

Plowed under every spring
And driven over
By giant combines every fall,
They are as one
With nothing to divide them,
Or to distinguish one from twenty others,
Now part of a larger farm.

"Who farmed this eighty?"
"Where was the Thomas barn
Or the Franklin place?"
"I don't recall."
"I could never find it now."
"I hope that Grandpa could
If he were here."

Reflections on a Farm Auction

Our neighbor had a sale
So he could move to town
To tend a garden,
Instead of fields and the truck patch –
To cut the grass instead of hay
And, when that was done,
To sit on the porch and drink lemonade
Before he took his nap.

I stood nearby and watched him
As they sold the farm off –
Piece by piece.

The tractor –
The first and last one he'd ever owned
Went first – bought new and shiny
When the horses grew too old and tired
To help him work.
I noticed the paint worn from the seat
and the patches on his overalls
From years spent together
Mowing, planting, harvesting.

The plow followed behind, as was its custom.
He wiped his brow and I saw the furrows,
Placed there by the sun,
As he toiled under its watch
Year after year,
As the seasons told him to.

His last saddlehorse
was led to a waiting trailer,
About the middle of the afternoon,
and I could see him younger,
Riding in the pasture, counting the cattle.

Wagons, rakes, and assorted tools –
The handles as smooth and worn
As his hands were gnarled and callused.
So, it went for hours
As I watched him watch,
Not alone, what was happening now
But also, what had gone before.

I watched him stand,
Straight as the pin oak out by the barn,
But with a little smile and a tear.
Friends and neighbors
Walked by, spoke briefly,
And carried away
The artifacts of his life's work,
But not the scars and aching joints and muscles.
Those, he got to keep.

Farm Toys

I don't recall a friend who had a pedal tractor
Who didn't live in town,
And drive it
On the sidewalk or the lawn.
Though I might have,
I don't remember wanting one.
We had the real ones
To ride on with our Dads
Or pretend to drive when they weren't being used.

We never imagined how many hours
We'd spend on them,
In just a few short years,
When we'd occupy our days
With mowing, raking,
Plowing, disking -
Harvesting oats - corn – hay,
Anxious to get off
And go to town.

The Dynamite Shed

It was just a small and rusted, corrugated shed
We called the dynamite shed
When Dad brought it to the farm
To store his Ford "N" tractor –
Nothing special except its story.

He'd bought it from my uncle
Who'd used it to store his chicken feed.
It was used to store explosives before that,
He told us,
At a construction site.

We fancied its former purpose
Much more than its recent ones
And relished sharing its story.
"Dynamite? Really? Awesome!
I wish we had one!"
We explained the bulge in the end
By an explosion,
Never giving thought
That any such blow
Would certainly
Have destroyed it totally.

Rust

Rust is nature's rebuke of our vanity
That the things we build of iron and steel will last.
The scavenger scours the fence rows, gullies
And the overgrowth
Behind the corncribs, chicken houses,
And the sheds that shelter new machinery.
It seeks the carcasses we leave behind –
Eats and digests
What the turkey vultures, the buzzards,
The beetles and the termites can't
And with its helpers, time and water,
Returns it to the land.

A Sub in the Pasture

"Ascend to periscope depth.
Up periscope!
Arm the torpedoes.
Flood tubes one and two.
Fire one! Fire Two!
They're throwing ash cans!
Down periscope. Dive!"

There was a water tank -
A concrete box beneath the ground
On the hill behind my best friend's house.
A windmill had been there once
Pumping water into it
Providing running water.
We'd never seen the windmill,
My friend or I,
And we'd only known the tank
To be dry enough to climb down in
When it hadn't rained for a while.

We hunted aircraft carriers
And cargo ships
With youthful abandon
From the pasture's depths
And recorded each kill
With a chalk mark on the concrete wall.
And when we'd finished our tour of duty,
We played baseball on the surface.

A Windmill's Lament

My name is "Aerometer"
Or so it says on my rusted vane,
Shot through with years
Of youthful target practice,
And now hanging by a single bolt.

I was proud once – and useful.
I stood in the pasture beyond the barn
And silhouetted myself against each dawn
To reveal to the inhabitants of the kitchen
How fast the wind was blowing
And from what direction.

Five decades –
Fifty years –
Eighteen thousand two hundred and fifty days,
I reached into the sky
With my tin fingers.
I caught each passing breeze – briefly,
Borrowed its power
To pump the farm's water
Then let it go upon its way -
To push along the clouds,
Rain, oat chaff, snow,
Or whatever else it found.

The kitchen is gone
So too, those who watched from the window,
And the barn.
Still I stand, but unwatched
Except by an occasional,
Unknowing, uncaring cow.
I no longer borrow from the wind
But whirl uselessly
At its whim, for its pleasure,
With my remaining fingers.

Lois' Garden

I drove by it often in the summer of '62
Or, rather, rode by with Dad
To and from town for a haircut
Or to buy feed for the hogs.

It had been Herb and Lois' home
For as long as either of us recalled
Until two summers before
When Lois died –
Four years after Herb.

Each time we passed,
It seemed the mulberry bush,
The morning glory,
And other climbing vines
Had enlarged their territory
At the porch's expense
Until now it was nearly hidden.

Lois' vegetable garden,
Lay beside the smokehouse
That endured for years
Beyond its purpose near the corncrib
And housed her trowels, rakes, and hoes.
Now two years unplanted, un-hoed, unpicked -
Its harvest not canned, nor frozen, nor eaten.

Tomato vines remained,
Though shrunken and brown,
Hardly visible
Held partly upright
Only by the surrounding weeds.

A few brown cornstalks stood,
Long stripped by squirrels,
Of their un-replenished bounty
And here and there survived
By a few green stalks -
Only distant cousins, unintended,
Of what she'd once planted.

Twins, Almost

The two were born two miles apart
To settlers
On the farms where each grew up.
They could have been twins
But though they weren't
They may as well have been.

Both turned forty
In 1910
And eighty -
In 1950.

The one was a willing farmer.
The other had a different dream.
Yet both were keepers of the land
And faithful servants of the soil.

Their land adjoined
As did their lives
For most of ninety years.

My friend and I
Were born just rooms apart
In the local hospital.
We could have been twins
But though we weren't
We may as well have been.
We turned ten years old together
In 1958
The year our grandpas died.

An Armory in the Stairwell

Most farms had an armory,
A necessary one,
To deal with predators -
Mostly with four legs
But occasionally with two.
Grandpa's was near the kitchen,
Just inside the cellar stairway door.

There were guns for butchering
A hog or steer,
Or to sadly ease the pain
Of a dog or mule or horse
Abused by time and wanting rest.

There were pieces for hunting too –
For sport and food
But never for sport alone,
A goose for Christmas dinner,
Venison for a different family meal.

Usually a rifle or two –
A boy's .22 for rabbits or squirrels
And an occasional windmill vane for practice –
And something more powerful
With longer range.
Always shotguns -
A boy's .410 for quail or doves
A 12 or 16 gauge
For larger fowl or game.

Cravings

The cravings consume my senses – sometimes.
My ears crave the "pop, pop, pop"
Of Dad's John Deere "B"
As it brings him from the field
With another load of hay
Or to the house for lunch.
They crave the midnight bawling
Of cows and calves,
Newly separated in autumn
By a gravel road
And two barbed wire fences.

My nostrils crave the smell
Of clover, alfalfa, and timothy
Freshly mowed and waiting
To be windrowed and baled.
They crave the smell of smoke
As it rises
From a crackling pile of leaves
In the middle of the garden –
A smoke that signals
The passing of summer,
The presence of mid-autumn
And the approach of winter.

My taste buds crave the sweetness
Of a pear just picked
At the end of the lane –
Not washed, just bitten into and chewed
As a reward
After walking home from school.

They crave the taste
Of fresh-fried side meat,
From a hog butchered at the farm,
Not store-bought bacon.

My eyes crave the sight
Of my Collie dog, Duke,
Swimming into the pond
To coax the recalcitrant Brown Swiss
Toward the barn for evening milking.
They crave watching our beagle
Happily chasing rabbits in the apple orchard
And the white wonder
Of snowflakes dancing before the yard light
On a January night.

My toes crave the squish
Of creamy soft mud between them
In the lane beside the barn
Where, before the rain,
There was powdery dust
Left by slides hauling hay bales.
My fingers crave the rough-sawn boards
Of the ladder to a hayloft
Full of adventures.

I lean back and close my eyes,
In the quiet of a room
Devoid of any scent.
My palate cleared of any taste.
Devoid of anything new.

I rest my hands
Across the denim of my shirt.
And let it all come back.

The Cat at the Gravel Pit

There was a big, yellow cat, I heard,
That lived at the gravel pit
A mile south of our farm –
Or it had before our time,
Before the pit was abandoned
To fishing
And to the weeds and brush and trees
That had overgrown its banks.

I fished there with my Dad,
Only once that I recall –
He with a rod and reel
And his only lure that I remember,
A Jitterbug -
I with a bamboo pole,
A worm and a cork.
I don't remember what we caught,
If anything at all,
Or remember seeing the cat –
Only hearing people talk of it.

I found the cat years later
While fishing with my brother.
The fish not biting,
Bored, we wandered into the trees and
brush –

Now years taller,
Now years denser.

We spotted it together
Peering from behind a stand of river Birch –
The lens from one headlight eye

Broken, filled with dirty water,
The other whole, but
Encrusted with years of grime.
Its grill had a Cheshire grin
But half its teeth were gone –
The rest stained reddish brown
Instead of yellow.

A familiar hood
Was camouflaged by leaves,
Themselves now yellow and orange.
Only **CATERPILLAR** showed though.

The Daisy Kid

I was an assassin,
A hired gun – a bounty hunter,
Whose mission
Was to rid the corncrib and the barn
Of rats and mice
And starlings and sparrows.

A penny apiece for the mice and birds –
A dime for the larger "game"
That I never got.

I was a sniper
When I was nine -
Hiding stealthily
With my trusty Daisy BB gun
In feed bunks
Or behind the bales of hay
Waiting for a target to appear
And aiming carefully
So as not to miss the shot
And scare it off.

One day an owl came
To live in the barn -
Followed shortly by a cat.
The quarry disappeared.
I turned to shooting soup cans –
And used my allowance
To finish paying for the gun.

Advice

There are things that Grandpa told me
Not long before he died,
That I'm glad he did.

"Don't buy the cheapest tools you find,"
He said, "And don't neglect the ones you have.
Buy once, buy well, and treat them right
They're yours.
Otherwise, you only rent them."

"You won't get taller
By climbing on someone else's back.
You may get up, even stay a while,
But soon they'll stumble
Under your weight.
You'll both fall down
And neither can help the other up."

"You spend your time and energy
complaining about something
And do it on and on,
And still not change it.
And even if you do,
You'll still not be happy
And will find a new complaint."

The Canons of the Farm

Work doesn't start
When the sun comes up
Or stop when it goes down.

We don't own the land-
It owns us.
We are only its keepers
While we're here.
It can be generous with its bounty
But a demanding master.

The stock and crops
Come before the people.
Without them,
The people don't eat.

We can neither bring the rain
Nor stop the wind and hail.
Each will come on its own time
And depart when it's ready.

We only get as good
As what we give.

Boys and button weeds
Are natural enemies.
Boys and dirt
Are friends for life.

To a calf,
A fence is merely a suggestion.
If you need to find
Which fences need fixing,
Follow the calves.

If the creek never floods,
The bottom-land never gets new soil.

A tractor seat is hard.
Going hungry is harder.

Sundays are for Church
And family dinners;
For calling on friends,
And rest.
Don't waste them working.

Chickens aren't pets.
They're stew and Sunday dinner.

The blade on a hoe
Is only as good
As the person holding the handle.

A milk cow in the barn
Is worth two
Standing stubbornly in the pond.

The job isn't done until
The tools are oiled and stored.

If the sign says "Beware of dog",
Beware of the dog.

The Reaper in the Weeds

They exhumed the reaper from the dirt
And the entangling Morning Glory,
Along the fence
Behind the tractor shed,
And for the first time ever
Rigged it to pull behind a tractor.

They brushed away the leaves and dust
And for the first time since it was laid to rest
"McCormick" saw the day.
Years of earth hard-caked the seat.
A long-abandoned bird nest
Rested where the twine
Was supposed to be
And an ancient wasp nest
Lay in the tool box.

The canvas had been rolled and saved
On top the rafters in the
Machinery shed
But most of the oak on the gathering reel
Would need to be replaced.

They wouldn't bother painting
And the aged metal wouldn't shine.
But they hoped that grease and oil
Would make the gears all work
For a run through the ripe oat field.

There wasn't time to waste.
The threshers would be coming soon
So the young could see and do it once
And the old for one last time.

I watched -
And carried water.

Reprinted from <u>The Horse Lawyer and Other Poems.</u>

The Sheep Pen Alamo

It was just a small pen made of stone
Along the lane behind the barn.
My grandfather, or his father before him,
I'll never know which,
Had put it there to hold the sheep.

My friends and I
Called it the Alamo
For it was the closest thing we had
That resembled it.

We'd gather inside
With coonskin caps,
Toy muskets, and wooden swords
And waited for the foe to emerge
From their encampment
In the soybean field.
The gate to the pen was long-since gone
But it was just as well.
It made a spot to place our cannon –
A fence post laid across a set of wheels
Taken from the scrap iron pile
Behind the chicken house.

Unlike the brave defenders
Of the ill-fated fort,
We survived to fight again
Even after the wall had been breached.
We'd fight the make-believe enemy
And force them to retreat.
We'd unwrap and eat the sandwiches
Our Moms had made, then wait
Beside our fencepost cannon
For the imaginary foe to come again.

Bluegrass

A Walmart stands now,
Where once
There was a bluegrass collection yard
At the edge of town --
Shame.

It wasn't a bluegrass lawn
But a gathering field,
Where local farmers
Brought the annual crop
To be threshed out
And sold for its seed.

No bluegrass bands or music
Disturbed the air,
Only the hum of tractors –
Hauling fresh-cut grass,
Raking head-high windrows
To feed the green and orange combines.

They only used it once a year,
For a while during harvest,
Which was good for the town.
It provided a picnic ground,
A place to play ball,
And watch fireworks on the fourth.

"Progress," the town fathers said,
When the new store came to town.
Sometimes I don't like progress very well.

A Marker in the Lane

Our neighbor's name
Was never etched in stone
Above the doorway
Of a library or a civic building or a school.
It didn't appear at the gateway to a park
Or on a street sign.

He left no mark
On the fields he'd farmed –
Crops planted, tended, harvested,
Consumed or sold.
The stubble plowed under or disked
Disappeared into next year's work.

I walk the lane from the road
To where a house and barn once stood.
On a half-way post
A roll of rusted barbed wire
That he'd saved to one day patch the fence
Reminds me that he was here.

In the Harvestore's Shadow

For forty years,
It was the tallest structure on the farm –
Taller than the windmill
Just outside the feed yard,
Taller than the barn consumed
By fire years ago
During an August thunderstorm.

Forty years filled,
Forty years emptied,
Now fifty years
Unused but standing –
A red clay tower
Spends its afternoons
In the shadow
Of the big blue Harvestore
And a poplar tree
Grows through its top.

Stories from Minley

Author's Note

The town of Minley, Iowa doesn't exist. It never has, really. I made it up. But in a sense, it **is and was** real. It is any of hundreds of thriving small communities spread across the heartland between the end of WWII and the time when interstate highways, superstores, and school district consolidations consigned them to history. So too, are the stories of the people of Minley. These are a *blend* of those of many people, some of whom I personally recall, those whose stories that others have related to me, and some of people I simply think I would have found interesting.

I've put Minley somewhere between Mason City and Sioux City. You can put it wherever you remember it best. Welcome home.

Greg Seeley

Sammy Gunn

My name is Sam Gunn. I was born in the hospital in Sioux City and grew up on the farm that my parents shared with my grandparents, Benjamin Beebe Gunn and Ruth Anne Gunn, three miles south of Minley. My grandfather was named after his father, Benjamin and his middle name was his mother's maiden name. It was thus that he came to be known as B.B. Gunn.

From my earliest recollection to the time I headed off to Iowa State, I was always called Sammy to distinguish me from my dad who was 'Sam'. As a child, I often wished that my parents had named me 'Thomas' instead of 'Sam'. That way, I could have been called 'Tommy Gunn' which sounded both cool and tough. Or I would have settled for 'Raymond' after my mother's dad, Raymond Hammons, who lived in town. 'Ray Gunn' sounded nearly as enticing since I was both into gangster movies and "Commando Cody, Sky Marshall of the Universe." As it was, I was stuck with 'Sammy', which sounded neither tough nor cool. For some odd reason though, when 'Peter Gunn' came on TV in 1958 or 1959, I found myself relieved that my parents had not named me 'Pete' or 'Peter'.

Grandpa Ernie

I must tell you about Grandpa Ernie. Grandpa Ernie taught us about dying by dying. It was the summer of 1954. My friend Bob and I were six and Grandpa Ernie was – well, old. Bob and I had never known anyone to die. All of the old people we knew had been around forever and, as far as we knew, always would be – until Grandpa Ernie died.

Grandpa Ernie wasn't my real grandpa and he wasn't Bob's either. In fact, Grandpa Ernie had no grandkids of his own. He had no relatives at all in the town - or anywhere else as far as anyone knew. Since Bob had no grandparents of his own, he took to calling Ernie "Grandpa Ernie", which was fine with his parents. I took to doin' the same even though I had two grandpas. Soon the other kids started calling him Grandpa too. Then before long everyone in town was calling him Grandpa Ernie.

No one seemed to remember for sure when Grandpa Ernie came to town. He told us kids that he didn't remember for sure either. He said he thought he was born in Mississippi but it might have been in Alabama and he weren't for sure when. Said his papa told 'm he'd been born a slave not long before the Yankees arrived 'n tol' all the folks on the plantation they wuz free. Told us about his papa bein' a sharecropper – said he didn't remember his mama. Grandpa Ernie told us about followin' his pa as he plowed cotton fields with a mule. Said his papa tol' him that bein' a sharecropper wasn't much different than bein' a slave 'n how once you got in debt to the landowner you could'n any more leave than if you wuz one.

We asked Grandpa how it was that he ended up in Iowa and he said one day when he just got big enough to learn to plow he was standing behind a mule. "I wuz a try'n all I could to get that ole mule to go north in the field and he jus' stood there like I was a post or sumpin'. He'd turn roun' 'n look at me between his blinders and heen' haw like he wuz a laughin' at me. I'd cuss 'im and he jus' laugh more 'n acted like he wuz a gonna start cussin' back. Don't you kids ever cuss now," he told us, "It ain't gentleman like n' your Mama 'd be right to wash your mouth out with soap 'n water. Anyhows, that mule decided he weren't gonna walk north 'n plow that day 'n I kep' tellin' 'im he wuz. Finally, I tol' 'im if you ain't gonna walk north then I am. I jus' left him standin' there 'n I started walkin' an' that's how I ended up in Iowa.

I learned much later that Grandpa Ernie had given the adults a much different account of his early life – an account far less suitable for the ears of small children. He had indeed been born a slave, though he had never really explained to us as children what a slave *was*. That's pretty much where the two stories diverge. After the war, he had grown into his teen years as the son of a sharecropper on a farm not far from the plantation where his father had labored as a slave. He didn't remember his mama – he figured she'd died when he was five or six years old.

When Ernie was perhaps fifteen or sixteen – he didn't really recall, he had gone to the house of a neighbor to borrow some small tools. It was about the time that a local farmer's house had been burglarized and some of the silver taken. Ernie figured the locals must have thought his pa had done it since, when he got home, he found their cabin burned to the ground and his pa's body hanging in a nearby tree. As Ernie told it, he took some canvas from the shed that hadn't been burned, buried his pa in a little apple grove behind where the house had been and left.

Ernie's first job had been sweeping floors at a little store run by a colored man -- that's what he called him, a *colored* man – somewhere south of Memphis. Eventually, the man's wife had taught him how to cook and he had moved to working in her kitchen in the café next to the store. He had it pretty good, he figured – room and board and a little bit of spending money to boot. But as he had grown a little older, he had begun to dream of something bigger. One day, a visitor came to the café. He was the conductor of a train that had stopped at the nearby depot and he had a problem. His cook had gotten mad and quit, leaving a group of hungry passengers in the dining car – growing impatient and not knowing that no food was forthcoming. Could he get some food at the café and take it on the train? "No," he had been told. "We just served dinner and we're out of nearly everything." When asked who did the cooking, the wife pointed to Ernie.

"Are you a good cook?" the conductor had asked. When Ernie assured him that he was, the man asked him if he could ride the train the rest of the way to Little Rock and cook the food already on the train. He would hire a new cook in Little Rock, pay Ernie a tidy sum for his time, and make sure he got a free ride home. Ernie got on the train and cooked dining car food for the next thirty-five years.

Sometime around 1920, as Ernie recalled, the train on which he was working stopped at Minley, Iowa to take on coal and water and to switch to a replacement crew. Ernie and the rest of the crew would wait a couple of hours and then catch the next train going the other direction. That was when Ernie decided to take a little walk about town. Not knowing how the people of Minley would react to a colored man, he decided to take a chance. He stepped out of the depot and headed uptown.

A week later, Ernie was back in town and never cooked another meal on a train. Told us when he first set foot in Minley, everyone he met was so friendly like that he'd decided then and there that his railroadin' days were over. He'd gotten back on the train, cooked meals for the folks headin' to Sioux City and given his notice. Said he saved up enough from cookin' all those years to take his little railroad pension and open hisself a café right there on the east side of the square.

Anyhow, he told us, folks started flockin' to his establishment like flies to a pot of honey left open on the back porch. Since he didn't have a lot of room, folks quit waiting for the noon whistle on top of the water tower to go off and started comin' in at eleven-thirty to beat the rush. Then some folks allowed they oughta' come at 11:15. When the druggist next door retired and closed up, Ernie rented the space to put in more tables. When the folks traveling through on the trains started to get wind of how good Ernie's food was, those who had time began to come uptown to eat at Ernie's Place.

Ernie kept on serving up that food for twenty-five years. Said he had wanted to quit earlier but then when the war come along, G.I.s who had a little time to spare while the train was coaling started comin' in. Kept tellin' him how they liked gettin' food like they were used to havin' at home 'n he just couldn't quit. Finally, when the war ended, he decided to sell the place to the first returning vet. who wanted it and knew how to cook.

But, in Grandpa Ernie fashion, he didn't sell it. He *gave* it to Timothy Wilkers – all of it, the tables, the chairs, the stove – everything, even the recipes. All he asked was that Timothy continue to call it "Ernie's Place", which Timothy was more than happy to do, until Ernie died.

And, since Ernie wasn't going to have much money, could he eat there free for the rest of his years and stay living in his little apartment above the restaurant? Timothy quickly agreed to this also. Ernie stayed on for a while, helping Timothy learn the business and the recipes.

Even with little money, Ernie always had candy and other little treats for us kids. I suspect now that most of it was donated by Wally Henderson from the candy counter at his market – probably cut into his sales a bit but I think he did it for Grandpa Ernie, not for us. Grandpa spent most of his time, when the weather was nice, sitting on a park bench – it has a plaque with his name on it now – near the bandstand and not far from where the county courthouse used to stand. He'd sit there, even though he would have been more than welcome to sit with the retired men on the bench in front of the filling station. He'd sit there smokin' his pipe and nearly always had kids around and was always tellin' stories. Once, when we asked him why he didn't sit with the other old men, he scratched his head a while, then stroked his white whiskers, took a puff on his pipe, and then grinned. "I reckon I'd rather spend my time with you all. Maybe sometime, when I'm old and you're all grown up, maybe then I'll go sit with the old men." He had to be ninety or ninety-one but perhaps he really *didn't* feel old.

But Grandpa Ernie *was* old. One day, a couple of weeks after he had ridden with the mayor in Minley's Old Settlers Festival Parade, we went to the park and there was no Ernie.

When we went home and told our parents they said that, no, Ernie would not be at the park anymore. Ernie had died. When we asked what "died" meant, we were told that Grandpa Ernie had gone to live with Jesus. Instead of being relieved, I was instantly mad at Jesus. After all, Grandpa

67

belonged to *us kids*. Why would he leave us to go live with Jesus? When Mom said Ernie didn't have a choice, it really didn't help. It just made me madder at Jesus that He had taken him. "Will Grandpa Ernie give him gum and candy?" I asked.

"I imagine he will," I was told. "Ernie loved him."

"Did he love him more than he loved us?" Mom had to be getting really uncomfortable, I decided much later.

"Not more," she explained, "just differently."

I remember that I let it go at that point. I thought I was too big to cry so I went to the barn and crawled up into the haymow and cried *there*.

A couple of days later, our whole family and Bob's family and nearly every other family in town gathered for Grandpa Ernie's funeral. None of the churches in town or even the high school gym was large enough to accommodate everyone who wanted to come so it was decided to hold the funeral at the park. The weather was nice and it seemed appropriate since the park was Ernie's favorite place.

As I said, there was a bandstand near Grandpa Ernie's bench where members of the high school band would sometimes hold concerts on Saturday evenings. The bandstand, as I remember it, was a large wooden structure with a green roof. There was railing all around it with fancy white trim work. There was a wide set of stairs on each side. I'm not sure why there were two but there were. Before the service, Ernie's casket was placed on a platform on the bandstand with the lid open. People stood in line talking quietly among themselves as they waited to go up one set of stairs, pause for a moment over Ernie, and then descend the other stairs.

I remember asking Dad as we waited in line what everyone was doing. "We are waiting to see Grandpa Ernie," he informed me. Now I was really confused.

"Mom said Grandpa Ernie wasn't coming to the park anymore," I informed him. "She said he went to live in Heaven with Jesus."

When we got to the casket, Dad picked me up so I could see Grandpa Ernie one last time. "That isn't Grandpa Ernie!" I think I shouted, still confused, but yet somehow relieved. Indeed, the person in the casket didn't look at all like Grandpa Ernie. First of all, he wasn't smiling. I had never seen Grandpa Ernie without that wide smile. Second, he was wearing a dark blue suit with a carefully knotted tie. I had never seen him in a suit and tie. Still, I reached into my pocket, removed a piece of wrapped hard candy, and, just in case, dropped it on the man's chest where I suspect it remains to this day.

And that's how Grandpa Ernie taught us about dying. "Rest in peace, Grandpa Ernie."

A Small-town Life Well-lived

Clarence Small made his living selling drugs on the northeast corner of the square near the Farmers' Feed and Gain. No one complained and he was never arrested. Clarence owned the Rexall Store with its bright blue and orange sign. He also sold the school books that parents bought for their kids in country school – and their paste, their crayons, their pencils and their 'Big Chief' Tablets. And there were magazines and comic books on a wire carousel rack.

In the back of the store, Clarence filled prescriptions from the physician upstairs who shared an office "suite" with the dentist. Near the pharmacy counter, Clarence sold Pittsburgh Paints, mixing the colors with the same care that he used in dispensing medicine. If you were between five and eighty-five, Clarence's drug store was the social center of Minley. Our parents' generation had occupied the stools, tables, and booths at the soda fountain on Saturday evenings or before or after games. So did we, years later – same booths with our parents' initials sometimes carved in them - same stools, same tables, same Clarence mixing malts and shakes.

Clarence also sold gum and candy and cigarettes – as well as pipes, cigars and chewing tobacco. After all, it was legal in 1956 and even pharmacists and doctors were yet to learn of the harmful effects of smoking and chewing. Clarence knew my grandfather and would allow me to bring 50 cents from him and take him a can of Redman chewing Tobacco. Try *that* today with an eight-year-old.

Clarence loved kids in the same way a dad or grandpa does but had none of his own to congratulate when they won or to console when they lost – or to gently or teasingly admonish when he saw them going wrong. I never heard him criticize or speak ill of anyone, though I'm sure he was sometimes tempted. And if a kid came up a nickel short, he could still get candy or a Coke. Clarence also organized toy drives and food drives and clothing drives. He played Santa Claus for the Christmas parties at the County Home and the elementary school and made sure that everyone got some sort of gift. He needed only the hat, the red suit, and the beard. Everything else was all Clarence – the padding and the genuine "Ho, Ho, Ho!"

The store was the depot for Trailways, the only bus line serving Minley. Clarence would sell you a ticket, visit while you waited for the bus or leave you alone if you wanted. Then, he would escort you to the bus, tell you goodbye, and wave as you left. He would be the first to welcome you when you arrived home, carry your suitcase into the store, and give you a quarter for the payphone and a Coke to drink while you waited for someone to take you home.

It was on one such occasion that I learned more about Clarence than I had ever before imagined. To that point, I always assumed that he had been born somewhere in the vicinity of Minley, grown up there, and quietly spent his entire life there except for time spent away at college and pharmacy school. It had just begun to snow when Dad brought me to town to catch the bus back to college after Christmas break. The weather forecast had predicted little more than minor accumulation and I expected my wait as well as the ride back to school to be quite uneventful. I don't remember if it was my sophomore or my junior year. It doesn't matter. Anyhow, feeling particularly wealthy, I declined Clarence's offer of a quarter and purchased my own cherry Coke.

It was late afternoon and the clouds and snow made it begin to get dark even earlier than was normal for that time of year. Clarence and I were the only ones in the store. I was sitting on a stool at the soda fountain sipping on my Coke, and he was cleaning the malt machine.

The wind had picked up and the snow had begun falling harder. Before long, it was difficult to even see the city park across the street. We both wondered if, perhaps, the weather forecasters had gotten it wrong. I wasn't long before Clarence received a phone call. The bus had hit heavier snow. It wasn't snowbound but would be running about an hour and a half late. I was already beginning to become bored. Just trying to start a conversation to pass the time, I asked what I would now consider to be a very personal and inappropriate question. "So, Clarence, what happened to your leg?"

You see, Clarence had a profound limp. Most people who were around him had long-since grown accustomed to it and barely noticed but, for some reason, it had always intrigued me. I knew that my dad must have known but, somehow, I had never asked him. Now, here, I had asked. "I'm sorry. I shouldn't pry. It's none of my business."

No, it's okay. So, here's what happened. I didn't grow up in Minley – or even in Iowa, I was born in Princeton, Illinois in 1898. No jokes, OK? That must seem ancient to a youngster like you, he smiled. But that's fine with me. My dad was a farmer and Mom taught country school. You didn't need a college degree in that day. In fact, you didn't have to go to college at all and I didn't really plan on it myself. But they both insisted that I at least finish high school and so I did even though I sat out for a couple of years when Dad was sick and needed a lot of help on the farm.

72

Anyhow, as a kid, I always loved baseball. There wasn't anything like little league or anything like that, of course, but we did play softball at school during recess sometimes. At school, we had a real ball but just one. So, if it got lost in the weeds, we kept looking until we found it even it meant spending our whole lunch hour or even staying after school to hunt for it. And we had one bat. It was too big for the smaller kids and too small for the bigger ones but we made do. When we played at home, or on the school yard in the summer or on Saturdays, no one had a real ball. We made our own by soaking hedge apples in varnish to harden them and used pieces of scrap lumber for bats. Sometimes, of course, that hedge apple ball would just shatter when we hit it. We played baseball rules, pitching overhand and such. I remember taking one of Dad's worn-out leather work gloves and stuffing corn husks in it for a catcher's mitt. Man, did that itch!

Our high school didn't have a baseball team either. But some of the small towns around were beginning to organize town teams that would travel around and play each other. Most teams got the town merchants to outfit them with uniforms and some equipment in return for putting the town's name on the shirts. Each shirt also had the name of a particular merchant on it. Mine was **Hale Blacksmith.**

Clarence finished cleaning the malt machine and made a pot of coffee. We moved from the soda fountain to a booth.

Well, we travelled around the county and played. We were pretty good if I do say so myself. We won more than our share of games and got a pretty good following.

73

I had just finished high school and we were playing a home game against a team that had come all the way from Galesburg. Just before the game, we learned that a scout from the Chicago Cubs was going to be at the game that day to look at a pitcher from the Galesburg Giants. Well, I hit two doubles and two home runs off that hot-shot and caught him trying to steal second base. I don't recall if the Cubs ever signed him but, that evening, I was on a train with that scout on my way to Chicago for an official tryout. Two week later, I was with the Cubs' minor league club in Decatur to get 'seasoned'. I played two games with them just as the U.S. got into World War I. By September, I was in the army and on my way to France. The Cubs told me I would catch in Chicago when I got home. Ty Cobb had been my baseball idol growing up. I felt better about being away from baseball when I learned that he was in the army too. I looked forward to maybe playing against him when we got home if the Tigers and the Cubs ever met in the World Series.

I got assigned to a wagon company. My job was driving a team delivering weapons, ammunition, and food to the front. Often, if there weren't enough ambulances, we would return to the supply depot with a load of corpses or wounded soldiers. That was the worst part of the job. I liked horses and had driven a wagon nearly since I was old enough to walk but this was different. The noise, the smoke, the suffering. My God, the suffering! I could never have imagined the lengths that people who called themselves civilized would go to kill each other over a few square miles of mud! I felt lucky not to live in the trenches then have to crawl out to try charging down the German guns. But I was still scared every time we had to go to the front. I think anyone who wasn't scared was crazy.

He went up to the counter and came back with a doughnut for each of us. It had gotten completely dark out by now, except for a faint glow from the barely visible street lights, but we could tell that the snow was coming down even harder and the wind had picked up. *May need to make more coffee. Everyone on the bus may want coffee – if it even makes it this far. Phone line is dead now; won't know if they're coming until they get here.*

I asked him if he needed to go home. *Nah, Mary's in Sioux City visiting her sister. Might just as well be here.*

Well, I never got shot but I got wounded just the same – hospital, purple heart, discharge, and home. Can't say I missed the war but sure did feel sorry for the guys who were still over there.

"What happened?" I asked.

We were at the supply depot loading our wagon. I was standing between two wagons when a German plane flew right over us – came in low and loud. As I said, I was standing right between the wagons. The horses hitched to our wagon got spooked and bolted. The wagon lurched forward and caught my knee right between the wheel hubs of the two wagons and crushed it.
Next thing I knew, I was in an ambulance headed for the hospital at the rear. Anyhow, the docs knew they couldn't fix it and they were about to just take it off. I begged them to leave it so they just set it with a splint and I never bent it again. Of course, I never played baseball again either. I did go to Chicago a couple of times though when the Detroit Tigers were in town and got to see Ty Cobb play in person. Someone from the Cubs must have told someone with the White Sox about me. At one game, when the Tigers came to town to play the Sox, I got to go out on the field

and play a little catch with him. He autographed the ball and gave it to me along with a signed bat.

So anyway, I could still pitch hay and drive a wagon so, after I was discharged, I went back to the farm. When my little brother got big enough to help Dad with the farm, I headed off to the University of Illinois and became a pharmacist. You pretty much know the rest.

The bus eventually arrived about four hours and two pots of coffee later. Clarence and I talked about many other things but I don't remember any of them. I remember only that I was probably the last person to see him alive. He must have stayed at the store the rest of the night. The next morning, Doc Savage found him lying on the sidewalk in front of the store next to his snow shovel. Clarence had the biggest heart in Minley. Sometime in the early morning, it just quit on him.

Dick's Diner
(Midway)

Midway was even smaller than Minley. No one I ever talked to seemed to know why it was called Midway. It was not midway between Sioux City and Mason City. It was not midway between Minley and any of the surrounding communities. In fact, it was not midway between any recognizable points of interest at all. To call Midway a town was as generous as calling Minley a metropolis. Minley had a stoplight. Midway had no stoplights because it had no streets – only the highway upon which one could go east or west. That's unless you counted the alley that ran about a hundred yards from the back of the gas station to Dick Bromwell's house.

Some of the old-timers remembered Midway as a thriving community with a railroad junction, a hotel, a general store, a blacksmith shop, and, before prohibition, a saloon. By the time I remember it, the "town" consisted of the aforementioned gas station and house, Dick's Diner, Dick's wife, Myra's, two-chair hair salon (creatively named Myra's), a retired semi-trailer (minus the tractor and with the name "F. W. Woolworth" barely showing through the rust) that sat along the alley behind the station, and the sale barn. Dick and his wife owned all of it except the sale barn. Since Midway had long-since ceased to be incorporated, Dick served as mayor and police chief. Dick and Myra together made up the town council.

Since Dick had never been able to reach any kind of franchise agreement with any major oil company, he was an independent jobber. He had named his station "Dick's Gas" and had placed a sign facing each direction about half a mile away from town stating simply "Eat and get gas at Dick's." Since Dick couldn't pump gas, wash windshields, and hand out Green Stamps while running the diner at the same time, he had hired Myra's forty-something cousin, Hubert, to pump gas, wash windshields, and hand out Green Stamps while he manned the grill at the diner. Hubert's sister, Sharon, meanwhile, waited booths, the one table, and the counter. During busy times (sale day) Sharon's sister, Susan, helped out.

In spite of privately making fun of the road signs, everyone in and around Midway liked and admired Dick Bromwell. He was a decorated Marine in WWII, going ashore in the first waves at both Iwo Jima and Okinawa and served in the honor guard at the VFW in Minley. Dick had always thought he would like to own a restaurant. As a boy, he had worked for a time sweeping floors and bussing tables at Ernie's Place where his mother had worked as a waitress. He had thought about buying Ernie out when he came home from the war but, by the time he got home, Ernie had already made other arrangements. He had also always enjoyed working on cars. "I can always get my hands greasy doing one or the other," he liked to joke. So, when the opportunity came along to purchase the entire town of Midway, he had gone to the bank, gotten a loan, and set about getting his hands greasy.

We had driven by Dick's many times when traveling back and forth to Fort Dodge or Sioux City, sometimes stopping at the station for gas but I had never set foot inside the diner until the spring of 1962 after I had turned fourteen and graduated the eighth grade. Even when we went to Midway for the livestock auction, we had always eaten in the lunchroom at the sale barn. I never asked him even later whether it was the beer he didn't want us to see or the talk that he didn't want us to hear. After all, I had seen my uncle drink *Schlitz* that he brought to family picnics and I had already heard most of the words at school. Anyhow,

78

I'll never forget that first tenderloin I had at Dick's. At the risk of a very bad pun, it was hog heaven. Iowa was famous for its pork tenderloins even then and Dick's were among the biggest and best – even better than what you could get at the state fair. Add in the fries served with them in a plastic basket and wash it all down with an ice-cold Coke and what you had was unbeatable!

To say that Dick's Diner wasn't fancy is a gross understatement. The building was a small, grey cinder block structure with a faded green asphalt shingle roof and a red front door with a window on either side. Over the door was a bracket sticking out toward the highway from which hung a lit sign proudly advertising Hamm's Beer. In each window was a neon sign – one promoting Schlitz and one pushing Falstaff. The Budweiser ad was on a neon clock hanging on the wall facing the lunch counter. The floor of the establishment was faded black and white linoleum, many of the square tiles missing a corner and displaying the aging plywood subfloor. The walls were paneled with knotty pine that had long-since lost its luster and was covered with pictures and other memorabilia from Dick's Marine Corp days.

The benches in the booths were covered with the same faded and scratched red vinyl as the tables, chairs and the counter stools. That was the only part of the place's décor that appeared matched. The free-standing tables and those at the booths sported red gingham oil-cloth covers topped with red and yellow squeeze bottles for ketchup and mustard.

Just inside and to the right of the front door was a cigarette vending machine containing various brands – Camel, Kool, Kent, and others. Anyone could use them. No one ever checked IDs. Products purchased could be used right there in the café as a condiment for beer, Coke, or coffee.

On the other side of the door was a juke box that featured only country music – Dick's favorite. For a nickel, one could listen to Hank Williams (Not Hank Jr.), Roy Acuff, or Patsy Cline. If you wanted Buddy Holly or Elvis Presley, it was necessary to drive to Minley or to one of the drive-ins in Fort Dodge or Sioux City.

Myra normally closed the hair salon from 11:00 to 2:00 on Friday (sale day) to assist Sharon and Susan in waiting tables. It was necessary to have three waitresses in the little establishment due to the amount of time Susan and Sharon each spent flirting with the male customers. Sharon and Susan carried order pads in the pockets of their aprons – not Myra though. Myra would patiently listen to each order, writing down not a word, and would then return having filled each order perfectly.

Dick could easily visit with any customer in the place without ever leaving his place at the grill. The grill was behind the lunch counter and Dick had arranged it so that he could cook facing the counter rather than standing with his back to it. The lunch counter was all that separated the grill from the "dining room". Dick would stand over the grill turning steaks, hamburgers, and pork tenderloins as quickly as his customers could order them without ever missing a beat while at the same time smoking Camels and swilling coffee.

Dick's Diner was the only establishment I recall from those days that appeared equally inviting to teens and middle-aged as well as aging farmers with three-day whiskers. Talk ran the gamut from the weather and the price of soybeans to "kiss and tell" stories that I decided later probably involved much more "tell" than "kiss". The stories I recall were generally good-natured and accompanied by laughter but far from what would today be considered "politically correct."

"I was out with Cathy Sheller Saturday night at the drive-in in Fort Dodge. We were watching the movie and she was all close up to me and I got my hand inside her sweater." (Truth moment – he did indeed get his hand inside of Cathy's sweater but she was not wearing it. She was wearing a jacket, not a sweater, and the sweater was draped over the back of the car seat).

"I ran into Charlie Harper the other day at the John Deere Store in Minley. Charlie had just gotten back from Omaha. He told me he saw these two guys walkin' down Farnham Street. He said they was holdin' hands right out there in fronta' God and everyone and then they …" Sorry folks, I can't share the rest of this one.

"Saw the damndest thing the other day. I don't think Pete Stalker would mind me tellin'. He was laughin' so hard hisself after it was over I thought he was gonna piss 'is pants right there and then. I went to his place to borrow his chainsaw to cut up this old elm tree that had fallen in my south pasture. You remember that tree? It's the one by the windmill that you 'n me scrambled up onto that time when we was teasn' Dad's ol' Angus bull 'n we made him so mad he commenced to chasin' us. How old were we? Six maybe? Anyhow, I was over there 'n he was at the corncrib a shoveln' corn inta his corn grinder. He was a shoveln' and his ol' Johnny popper was jus' a poppin' away and makin' a racket 'n I walked up behind 'im and grabbed 'is shoulder 'n yelled 'look out', Pete! Well anyway, ol' Pete, he just about jumped outta 'is Big Smiths. Hell, that ain't even the best part. Just then, that corn grinder started makin' this horrendous noise. That thing was a rattlin' 'n a schreechin' somethin' terrible like I never heard before. Anyhow, I started runnin' toward the tractor to shut it off but Pete jus' stood there like he thought if he stared at it hard enough it would stop its screechin' 'n go back to workin' like normal. Anyhow, jus' before I got to the tractor, I heard this tremendous boom 'n I turn around to see what done it. Damn if that ol' corn grinder hadn't blowed up on 'im. He wasn't hurt or nothin' but he was just standin' there 'n he was all covered up from head to foot with corn dust 'n he opened his eyes 'n all I could see of the real Pete was 'is eyeballs. Soon as I knew he wasn't hurt I started laughin' and pretty soon Pete, he started laughin', and pretty soon we both started laughin' so hard we could'n stop. Anyhow, Helen, of course she came runnin' from the house as soon as she heard the boom 'n as soon as she saw we wasn' hurt she started laughin' too. Then she said 'Pete, you ain't comin in my clean house like that. You two, go over to pump 'n, Wilbur, you get 'im cleaned up. But don't do it yet. I

gotta go the house 'n get my camera. Doris
is gonna wanna put this in the paper!"

I don't recall exactly when Midway disappeared but I
remember driving by one time on a visit home and the
station, the diner, the hair salon, the semi-trailer, and the
house were all gone. All that remained was the sale barn –
and the signs along the highway. Pity.

Robby's Story

Robby Nelson was his own special gift to Minley. Most towns had a Robby. I hope that most towns loved their Robby as much as kids and grown-ups alike in Minley loved ours.

Robby was what you would call today a special-needs child. In that day, no one called them that. They didn't call them anything. It was just the way Robby was. It was sad, little more.

The one person in town who didn't feel bad about Robby's condition (other than the town bullies, Ben and Billy Barnum) was Robby himself. Robby, who in his nearly thirty-five years, had advanced little beyond the mental age of six, was, quite likely, Minley's happiest citizen. Robby had never learned to be cynical or anything but totally honest and trusting. He always had a smile to brighten someone else's day because he rarely had a bad day of his own and usually had a little joke that he had just learned and wanted to share with every person he met.

Ben and Billy weren't home-grown bullies. To my recollection, Minley had none of those – not serious ones anyhow. There were a few wannabes, whoever felt especially tough on a particular day, but they never bothered Robby. They had their standards and never considered him fair game. In fact, they picked mostly on each other. I never saw one of them send anything but a friendly laugh in his direction – with him, in response to one of his jokes, not at him, and I never heard them make fun of him even among themselves. They would sometimes escort him across the highway that separated his world from the elementary school playground and allow him as many swings as it took to hit the ball back past the pitcher and then gently escort him to first base.

Ben and Billy, on the other hand, were what you would call, I guess, "imports." They were about three years or so older than I and moved to Minley the year our country school closed and we farm kids began riding the bus to town. They had come from one of the less desirable parts of the big city of Cedar Rapids when their dad took a job as a route driver, picking up milk and eggs from the local farms for the Farmers' Co-op Creamery just north of town.

Anyhow, as I mentioned, Robby lived with his dad in a little two-bedroom house just across the highway from the elementary school. None of us ever knew what had happened to his mother. We certainly didn't ask Robby and he probably would not have known. I assume that some of our parents knew but they never volunteered the information and we didn't ask them either. It wasn't something that mattered a great deal except that we felt sorry for him that he didn't have a mother. It was just the way it was and we would have treated him no differently had we known.

Robby's world was not a lot larger than his small yard though his dad would bring him "uptown" occasionally for a malt at Clarence Small's drugstore, to see the Christmas decorations, or to a Saturday night ice-cream social hosted by the VFW or the Lions Club. Robby's little world was not fenced even though it was near the highway. It didn't need to be. One thing that Robby had learned years ago was never to leave the yard, even to chase a ball or to run to the playground. Never – unless accompanied by someone whom he knew and would look after him.

One afternoon – I think it was in spring, about the time we were finishing our first year of school in town – we had just gotten on the bus to go home. Several of us were sitting near the front of the bus and could see Robby's little world. As was customary for Robby at that time of day, he was in his yard so the kids on his side of the bus could wave and shout back and forth to him. He was standing there, wearing his blue bib overalls and his ever-present smile as big as all outdoors

As we were watching, Ben and Billy, who lived in town and so didn't ride the bus, came up to Robby. Ben grabbed Robby's football and tossed it to Billy. It didn't take long to realize that they weren't playing catch with Robby but were playing keep-away from him. It took a bit for Robby to realize what was happening but, as he did, the smile began to disappear. Billy walked up to Robby and started to hand him the ball but then pulled it back and held it above his head where Robby couldn't reach it. As he lowered it again, we could see that Ben was now on his hands and knees behind Robby ready for Billy to shove him. We could see that Robby was protesting and wanted his ball back but, of course, we knew it wasn't going to happen.

The older boys on the bus saw it too. Ken, our bus driver, saw it. The boys got up and started up the aisle from their seats heading toward the bus door. Ken saw them in his mirror and gave them a knowing glance and an approving nod. Next, he inched the bus forward to a spot where Robby's yard could not be seen from the principal's window at the school. There, he stopped the bus, opened the door, and allowed Dale and Tim to exit. Dale and Tim never talked about what they did to Ben and Billy. Neither did any of the witnesses on the bus. Ben and Billy, of, course, weren't going to tell anyone. Whatever happened, it must have been convincing. To my knowledge, Ben and

Billy never bothered Robby again in the two years before they moved away from Minley. I'm quite certain that they also gave Dale and Tim a wide berth whenever they saw them.

After I graduated high school and went off to college, I don't recall that I ever saw Robby again. We kids who were now out of school hung out together over summer break but normally didn't go to the ice cream socials and didn't include Robby. Robby didn't seem to mind. He constantly had a whole new set of friends. I felt bad for a while that I hadn't gone back to see him but Robby and I weren't as close as the kids who lived in town and were with him more often. I later decided that he probably would not have remembered me anyhow.

I don't know what happened to Robby later when his dad grew older and either died or was no longer able to care for the two of them. One of my friends, who had stayed in Minley, said that one day, Robby and his dad simply disappeared. He said he thought that they had moved to Red Oak to live with Robby's sister but wasn't sure. I hope Red Oak treated him well.

Charley's Motor Sales

Charley Davidson loved motorcycles – always had, he said,
ever since reading *Tom Swift and His Motorcycle* - loved
riding them and loved working on them. He joked that he
could have gotten rich and famous doing it, too, if his
parents had only left that danged "C" off his first name.
"Oh, well."

When Charley got old enough to go into business for
himself, he wanted a dealership but Harley-Davidson
would not sell him a franchise. Minley wasn't big enough,
they had told him. There was already one in Fort Dodge.
Besides, "Charley Davidson's Harley-Davidson" just didn't
sound right. Indian Motorcycles wouldn't sell him one
either. "Charley Davidson's Indian Motorcycle Sales"
seemed too confusing. No other maker would touch him
either. So, Charley resorted to driving his 1932 Dodge
Pick-up around Iowa picking up used cycles that he could
fix up and sell under the name "Charley's Cycle Sales."
Even then, there wasn't much market and Charley was
barely able to pay his rent and eke out a living. But he lived
with his parents, had few needs, and liked what he was
doing.

Then one day, Sally Jean Hanson moved to town from
Sioux Falls to live with her sister. Sally Jean was older than
Charley and not especially pretty but Charley was
immediately smitten with her. Her dad rode bikes, she had
told him, and she really wanted one of her own. Well, that
was enough for Charley. They started going out together to
ice-cream socials in the park on Saturday nights and riding
bikes around the county's back roads on Sunday
afternoons. But Charley still lived at home and most of
their meals together were in Charley's mother's kitchen
with Charley and his mom and dad and Sally sitting around

the same table eating pot roast. Once in a while, if Charley had made a really decent profit on selling a bike, they would eat at "Ernie's Place" or share a malt at Clarence Small's soda fountain.

It didn't take long for Charley (with Sally Jean's help) to realize that, if he wanted to keep her, something would have to change. So, Charley set out to change something. His first stop was the Citizen's Bank of Minley where his meager savings were deposited. The first of eleven visits were essentially fruitless as his loan requests were rejected each time. But Charley wanted Sally Jean badly enough to keep going back. On the twelfth visit, Charley had a card to play that he hadn't had before. He came into the bank with a letter from Chrysler Motor Company stating that, if he could arrange financing, Chrysler would grant him a franchise to operate a dealership in Minley. And that's how "Charley Davidson's Chrysler-Plymouth-Dodge-DeSoto and Used Motorcycle Sales" was born. Charley located his new venture two blocks off the square where the city hall and volunteer fire station now stand.

Charley figured his good fortune was mostly due to a chance visit to Minley by a marketing vice-president of Chrysler Motor Company. The man had been traveling west from Detroit to San Francisco on business when his train stopped at Minley. There he had found a telegram waiting for him instructing him to return as soon as possible to Detroit. Having time to kill before he could catch another train headed east, he had wandered about Minley and chanced to drop in at Charley's Cycle Sales. He had noticed, he told Charley, that nearly all of the cars and trucks parked around the town square were Fords with a few Chevrolets here and there and he wondered why. Chrysler built a good product, he explained, and Charley agreed, noting how many miles he had put on his 1932 Dodge pick-up and that he had never had a problem with it. Chrysler's problem in Minley, Charley had explained, was that the town had a thriving Ford dealership but that to buy any of Chrysler's products or get any of them worked on, one had to go all the way to Sioux City or Fort Dodge. Anyway, Charley got his dealership and Sally Jean. Charley's life was good.

What Charley had not counted on was the Davidson family curse. It was, of course, not a real curse and Charley had pretty much dismissed it as just a case of generational bad luck that had run its course. Charley's father's bad luck had involved buying a local brewery in Albert Lea, Minnesota. For the first two years the venture had been quite successful. He made a good living for the family and looked forward to a promising future. During the third year, the Eighteenth Amendment was passed and prohibition ended the business. With all of the family savings tied up in the business, there had been no choice but to sell the brewery at a bargain price to a man wanting to refit it as a shoe factory. Shortly thereafter, he had moved the family to Minley and taken a job working in the local hardware store. Charley's father had not been the first in the Davidson family to experience the "generational bad luck." Charley's great uncle Horace had spent his life savings to purchase a buggy factory in Indianapolis that he had, coincidentally, opened on the same day that Henry Ford had opened his first assembly line to build Model T's.

As it turned out, Charley's generational luck was no different than that of his father or his great uncle. Dad had done well for a while and, in the beginning, people had purchased enough of Horace's buggies for the business to be reasonably successful As it had been for them though, things went well for a couple of years. True to the family tradition, Charley had proudly opened his new car dealership two years to the day before the Japanese attacked Pearl Harbor, effectively shutting down automobile manufacturing and sales for the next four years. Too old for the draft, or even to volunteer for service, and married with Charley Jr. at home, Charley moved the family to Kansas City. For the remainder of the war, he used his mechanical skills working at the bomber plant.

After the war, Charley moved Sally Jean and his boys, Charley Jr. and Jack, back to Minley. The building and sales lot, which had been converted to a lumber business, were again available. Charley bought it all and re-opened the dealership

It would be an understatement to say that Charley was not a striking figure – noticeable, just not striking. He was nearing sixty years old by the time we kids first knew of him. Charley was tall and thin – not just thin but awkwardly so. So thin was Charley that people wondered if Sally Jean had ever fed him a proper meal though she was nearly universally acknowledged as one of the best cooks in town. Charley had never been what you would call a fashion plate but Sally Jean always insisted that he wear a suit when working on the sales floor of the dealership. The problem was that Charley never knew from one minute to the next whether he would be flat on his back underneath a Plymouth or out front selling one. So, he kept a suit coat and tie hanging on the back of his office door. If a customer came in for service and he had been working on a car or bike, he would slip into the office and emerge moments later wearing the same grease-stained trousers and shirt but now sporting the suit coat and tie. Suit coats that fit Charley's gangly frame were hard to find and the too-short sleeves made his arms look longer than they should have been. I doubt he ever re-tied the tie. It always appeared that he kept it tied but loose enough to put on over his head and just kept it that way, not bothering to tighten it once he had it on.

Charley shaved just often enough to keep Sally Jean from grabbing him by the ear and dragging him into Leo's Barbershop. He liked haircuts not much better. So, Charley normally had two or three days of white growth and long, but increasingly thin, white hair. In short, Charley was a man living just on the fringe of "Sally Jean's law."

Charley would sometimes ride his motorcycle, which he called "The Beast," while wearing the suit coat and tie. He didn't wear a helmet as we know them now but, instead, wore a leather aviator's helmet with goggles that he rarely pulled down over his eyes. As he rode, the over-sized suit coat would billow out under his arms like a pair of spreading wings. It was Robby, in the childlike innocence of his six-year-old mind in a thirty-something body, who first noticed what the rest of us had overlooked. We were on the school playground with Robby one day when Charley came roaring down the highway on "The Beast." The suit coat was flopping and flapping under his arms and the unfastened straps of that leather helmet were whipping about. Robby heard the noise and excitedly turned and pointed, "Look guys! Rocky!" All of a sudden, Robby had us all laughing uncontrollably. Of course, Charley couldn't hear us as we shouted after him, "Hey! You forgot Bullwinkle!"

And that's how Charley the Car Dealer became known to the kids of Minley as "Rocky." Whether Charley ever saw a "Rocky and Bullwinkle" cartoon or, if he did, he ever made the connection, will forever remain a mystery.

Homer Hayward's Hometown Hardware

Minley didn't have *Western Auto* or *Coast to Coast* hardware stores. Minley wasn't big enough. If you wanted either of those, you had to go to either Fort Dodge or Sioux City. What Minley *did* have was Homer Hayward's Hometown Hardware Store. Of course, no one in Minley ever called it that. It was simply "Homer's." If you needed nails or a new scoop shovel or a hammer or a saw, you went to "Homer's." It was that simple. "Homer's" sported a green, wood-framed screen door with a porcelain screen protector that proudly advertised BPS Paints. A sign painted on the glass in one of the large front windows proclaimed proudly, "Drop in or call. I'm always Home 'er here."

"Homer's" was not showy, even by the standards of the day. With a few exceptions, it was little different than it had been when Homer bought it from Homer Sr. after the war. Any varnish that had ever been on the pine floors had disappeared at least a generation ago leaving a dull gray residue that changed little in appearance after they had been freshly swept. No shiny metal or plastic shelves lined the bare brick walls – only wood ones on which were stacked rows of carefully tagged pasteboard boxes containing bulk quantities of nails, fencing staples, nuts, and bolts. Other merchandise simply sat in boxes on the floor.

Homer's store and the lumber yard were the last two establishments in town that, even in 1957, had not gone to oil as the fuel for their heat. In the back of the store, near where Homer sold plumbing pipe and duct work, stood a big, black stove in which Homer would burn either coal or wood depending on whichever was cheaper or more abundant at the time. Sometimes, cash-strapped farmers would pay for their merchandise in oak or elm from their timbers. That didn't help Homer pay his suppliers but it created loyalty among his customers and helped offset what it would otherwise have cost him to keep the store warm.

Above it all was that pressed-tin ceiling, re-painted every few years to keep the new rust from peeping through and to cover up the grime from cigarette, pipe, and cigar smoke.

Homer Hayward was not big on what we would now call merchandising. The counter where he rang up sales was not surrounded by racks containing "impulse" items. He had not laid out the store so that people had to walk by certain merchandise in order to reach other things they had come in to purchase. Stock was placed on the shelves where it would fit – not arranged in order to maximize sales. Garden seed might be placed near screws and nails if that's where it fit best – not next to rakes, hoes, and other garden tools. Everyone knew this and nearly all customers could walk right to what they needed in spite of the arrangement and rarely had to ask Homer, "Where do I find …?"

The basement of "Homer's" was nothing special from January through October. Each year though, about the first week of November, it became nearly the most fascinating and enchanting place in the world. Almost by magic, the drab gray space became a toy wonderland as Homer stocked it up for the Christmas season. Rows of nearly empty wood shelves to the right of the stairs became suddenly laden with all manner of trucks, tractors, bulldozers, coaster wagons, sleds, and air rifles. To the left, where I don't recall going, were the dolls, the doll houses, the baby carriages, and the tin, child-size kitchen appliances. Though not a merchandiser, Homer knew

94

enough to place fresh greenery to create just the right ambience and aroma. This was where he also sold his aluminum Christmas trees and color wheels. But the aroma I remember most did not come from the greenery. It came from all of that lead paint on the shiny new trucks and tractors. Of course, no one was worried about lead paint in the 1950's but, God, that smell!

In early summer of 1958, Homer acquired a franchise to become a *Gambles* hardware store. One Saturday, the familiar blue and white *Hayward's Hometown Hardware Store* sign came down and was replaced by an even larger *Gambles* green on white sign. Of course, everyone knew it was still *Homer's* but most almost immediately began to call it the *Gambles Store*. Homer had been reluctant to make the change but it gave him advertising advantages since *Gambles* now helped him with advertising costs and he could now carry merchandise exclusively available to *Gambles* dealers.

Of course, having just turned ten years old, I was totally unaware of any of the reasons for the name change and noticed little difference in the store other than the sign change. The one thing that I *did* notice about Homer's new *Gambles* line of merchandise was that new *Hiawatha* bicycle that appeared one Saturday just inside the front door. That was the most magnificent bicycle I had ever seen. First of all, it had 26" wheels. You see, I had started out with a rusty 20" bike that Dad had picked up at a farm auction. Not too much later, my friend down the road, whose legs were longer than mine, got a 24" bike. Of course, he needed a larger bike, but all of a sudden, my bike seemed woefully small and I almost immediately began to beg for a larger one. Fortunately, my little brother was almost big enough for a bike of his own. He got the 20" and Dad bought me a 24" from a neighbor whose son had graduated to a 26". That 24" served me well for a year or two until my friend grew into a 26". Then I began to want a 26". Still, my friend's legs were longer than mine and he needed a 26" while my legs remained comfortably suited to that 24" and I had to really stretch when he let me try riding his. That aside, I began to really want a 26" bike – and not a used one this time. I wanted a brand new one and the new one I wanted was that *Hiawatha*.

That *Hiawatha* 26" cruiser had it all. There were those magnificent tube-type whitewalls supported by the shiny chrome spokes. The front fender sported a chrome, two-beam headlight with matching trim on each side reaching down to the axle. Directly behind the handlebars with white rubber grips was a faux tank, which gave the look of a motorcycle but, of course, served no other purpose and simply added weight. Behind the seat was a chrome luggage rack where one could strap books during the school year or hang a pair of Roy Rogers Custom Deluxe genuine vinyl saddlebags. I had a boy crush like none I had ever felt before.

Every Saturday night when our family went to town that summer for ice-cream socials or Lions' Club barbecues, I made the *Gambles* store my first stop. I would go in there and stand by that bike and admire it and run my hands across that vinyl seat and the shiny fenders. "Sure is 'beaut," Homer would say and "She sure is," I would answer longingly.

Then one Saturday night in late summer, just as school was about to start, I made my usual stop at the *Gambles* store only to find that the love of my life was no longer there. "Yep, sold her," Homer told me. "Some guy came in a told me that bike was just about the finest he had ever seen and his son just had to have her." I had no idea who the man was and really didn't care but I was suddenly and insanely jealous of his son and began to wonder who I would see riding *my* bike around town.

Anyhow, the next morning, after Church and before lunch, Dad was reading the Sunday paper. I was sitting near him doing pretty much nothing but silently sulking over that bike. After a while, Dad looked up from the paper and asked me to go to the garage to get him a pair of pliers. I had never known anyone to need a pair of pliers to read the paper but I had nothing else to do so I got up and dutifully headed for the garage. I kept that bike for twenty-five or so years before trading it away. Kind of wish now I still had it.

Ronnie Rivers' West Side Tap

Ronnie Rivers' West Side Tap sat near Taylor's Market on, where else, the west side of the square in Minley. Ronnie's wasn't the cultural center of Minley but, to many of Ronnie's patrons, it had could have been and provided about as much culture as they felt they needed.

Ronnie's wasn't fancy. Few of the fixtures had been replaced or updated since before the war – not the wooden tables and chairs, not the bar, not the kitchen that served up a basic menu of hamburgers and cold ham sandwiches. The only two concessions Ronnie had made to the post-war era were the giant room-air conditioner that replaced the transom above the front door and a black and white Zenith TV that sat prominently behind the bar. The television, of course, received only the usual three channels. Much of the time the picture was either rolling upward more quickly than an out-of-control elevator or consisted of snow accompanied by static. Even so, it mattered little to the patrons. It was still as close as most had ever been to the Baseball Game of the Week and made them feel as if Dizzy Dean and Pee Wee Reese were bringing the game to them in person. Anyhow, Saturday afternoon was more about the beer and the conversation. The rest of the week, the TV sat mostly black and silent.

In the back room of Ronnie's were two of the town's only pool tables, the other two being in the basement of the newly-constructed VFW Hall. Six days a week, from open to close, the sound of pool balls rolling into one another, laughter, cursing, and crude jokes emanating from the room, punctuated the conversation at the bar. Hanging over the entire establishment was a constant cloud of cigarette, cigar, and pipe smoke. In the 1950's, the health warnings were years away. Few were even faintly aware of the dangers smoking presented. Of even less concern was what would later come to be known as second-hand smoke. All in all, Ronnie's was loud, hazy, blissful, and crude – just the way Ronnie and his band of regulars liked it.

Ronnie never worried about checking IDs from under-age customers. He knew his patrons personally. Most had been his customers since before the war. Ronnie also knew which of Minley's boys had either not yet graduated high school or had graduated too recently to partake of the goods. Besides, most of the younger crowd seemed to gravitate toward Dick's Diner over in Midway. Dick served up a small assortment of malts and shakes and a wider menu of food. For those who wanted a beer, Dick was more likely than Ronnie to accommodate them. Dick had a juke box. Ronnie had the mostly silent TV. Girls frequented Dick's but rarely came to Ronnie's.

Ronnie's regulars were mostly farmers and their hired men, retired farmers, or those who worked at the feed and grain. There were no baseball caps with team logos or hats worn with the bill toward the back and certainly no sunglasses. There were either straw hats or caps bearing the names "John Deere", "International Harvester", "DeKalb Seed," or "Pioneer". There were occasional pairs of Levi or Lee Jeans but the standard uniform was a pair of striped denim overalls bearing names such as "Big Smith", "Key Imperial", or "Osh Kosh B'gosh". Some wore work shirts underneath the overalls but many preferred either t-shirts or sleeveless ribbed-cotton undershirts. Often there was open space along the overall sides where the bib met the trousers that the undershirt gave way to an expanse of bare skin and a belly enhanced over time by too many beers and burgers.

The beers creating the enhanced bellies were not light. No one had heard of light beer and most would have equated it with slightly filtered pond water. Neither were there foreign beers – least of all German beers. The war was, after all, in the recent past – not a distant memory blurred by time and forgiveness. The Camel and Lucky Strike cigarettes were accompanied by beers made in Milwaukee or St. Louis – Pabst Blue Ribbon, Falstaff (Dizzy Dean's favorite), Schlitz, or Hamm's.

This is all, of course, hearsay. I was only in Ronnie's once that I recall, when I was, perhaps, nine or ten. My parents, as well as Grandpa and Grandma Gunn, were out of town and I had been left in the care of Grandpa Hammons, a retired farmer. It was a Saturday afternoon in the summer. Grandpa and Grandma Hammons did not yet have a TV at home and it was time for the Baseball Game of the Week so off we went. As chance would have it, there were two empty stools at the bar almost squarely in front of the Zenith. Grandpa Hammons helped me up onto one of the stools and promptly seated himself on the other. Grandpa ordered a Hamms or a Schlitz – I don't recall which. I had a hamburger and an Orange Nehi. My drink came with a straw but I quickly discarded it when I realized that I was the only one in the place drinking with a straw. I was big stuff, being at Ronnie's with the men. When Grandpa lit a Camel, I reached into my shirt pocket and pulled out a pack of candy cigarettes that I had purchased at Small's Drug Store when we first arrived uptown.

Grandma Gunn was mortified when she found out that Grandpa Hammons had taken me into what she called "That sin den." Grandpa Gunn and my parents also expressed their disapproval. Though, I think, they were silently and secretly a bit amused, they dared not let it show in Grandma's presence. I had to surrender the candy cigarettes but I don't recall being otherwise punished. The incident passed and, I don't think, was much remembered by anyone but myself and Grandma Gunn – she holding a grudge against Grandpa Hammons, me, a guilty pleasure.

Grandma Gunn, you see, had attended a temperance meeting when she was young and had signed a pledge to never drink liquor. It was an honorable thing but Grandma apparently read much more into the pledge than was actually there. I recall her telling me about the time that Grandpa Gunn and her sister's husband had brewed up a batch of homemade root beer and were sitting on the screened porch enjoying the results of their labor. While she hadn't scolded them, she told me, she had wanted no part of it herself since it had the name *beer*. As I mentioned earlier, Ronnie's West Side Tap was located next to Taylor's Market. Grandma bought nearly all of her groceries at Taylor's. If a parking spot was available directly in front of Taylor's, Grandma had no problem. If the only open spot happened to be in front of Ronnie's West Side Tap, she would refuse to park there, sometimes choosing the next open spot even if it was around the corner a block or more away. After all, she certainly could not have her friends see the car and think she had been frequenting "The sin den." Taylor's box boys would obediently, but I imagine, grudgingly, carry her purchases the extra distance. I hoped she tipped them but I doubt it.

All of this said, I reflect now on Ronnie's regulars. Almost to a man, these were the most honest and hard-working people on the planet. The rough talk was 95% bluster and the 5% that was an outright lie was tall-tale talk and everyone understood that. They were the first to jump in when *anyone,* whether part of their group or not, needed help harvesting or planting crops due to illness or injury. They would give the shirts off their backs without being asked. Saturday's coarse language was mostly confined inside the walls of Ronnie's West Side and not taken home or elsewhere. On Sunday it was almost universally replaced by prayer at one of Minley's five churches.

The John Deere Underground

Eric Petersen's friends called him "Little Swede" but never
to his face. When addressing him in person, he was simply
Eric – "Mr. Petersen" to us kids. By the same token, his
father, Paul, whose six-foot-one-inch frame was an inch
shorter than Eric's was "Big Swede" – simply by seniority,
and, again, never to his face.

Together, they had run Minley's John Deere dealership
ever since Eric returned from serving in the war. Paul had
run it long before that and had managed to keep the doors
open even through the years of the Dust Bowl and the
Great Depression. Unofficially, the farmers around Minley
referred to the establishment as "The Underground." One
hardly ever heard it referred to as its official name
"Petersen's John Deere." If a piece of equipment broke
during harvest, the farmer's wife would get in the pickup
and drive to The Underground for a part. When it was time
to replace a tractor or baler, the first stop was normally The
Underground.

I remember knowing that Little Swede had served in the
war, just as had nearly all of the able-bodied men of the
generation who lived in the county. This was true except
for those whose labor was needed on the farms to grow
food for the war effort. While some were quite open to
talking about their experiences in the war, others, like my
dad, simply wanted to try to forget most of it.
When we studied World War II in sophomore American
History class, several veterans were invited to talk to us
about the war. We never saw Little Swede. I always
assumed that he was one of those who simply didn't want
to talk about what he had seen and done. I found out later
that Little Swede had spent his entire tour of duty in

Nebraska guarding POWs and felt perpetually embarrassed that he had seen no action.

Anyhow, The Underground was uniquely situated. It sat directly across the street from Charley Davidson's Chrysler-Plymouth Dodge-Desoto and Used Motorcycle Dealership. The ground that it sat on was level with the street but then sloped steeply at the back allowing what we would now call a walk-in basement accessible from the alley that ran behind. Except it wasn't a walk-in but, rather, a drive-in. Tractors or implements could be driven or towed in through either of two giant garage doors that backed right up on the alley. Since the floor of the store itself was not concrete and could not support the weight of machinery, the showroom, such as it was, was also located in the basement alongside the repair shop. At most the "showroom" could hold two tractors or one tractor and another implement such as a disk, corn-planter, or a baler. I never saw a combine in there.

The street-level store was my favorite as I was growing up. There was, of course, the parts department. But, best of all, there was always a wide assortment of scale-model John Deere toys that ranged from tractors and wagons, to corn pickers and combines to balers. The Underground had pedal tractors, scaled-down versions of the newest and latest full-sized machines. I never had one. I never felt the need. By the time I was three, I would sit on Dad's lap on the real tractor. When I was seven, I would steer while he worked the pedals. At nine, I was driving our little Ford "N" while Dad stacked bales on a lowboy trailer pulled behind. But if someone purchased a new tractor, combine, etc., we kids always got the same thing in a free scale-model that we could play with in the house or in the sand-pile. One time, a neighbor who did earthwork such as ponds and drainage ditches bought a bulldozer/crawl tractor. He had only daughters but took the scale-model crawler anyhow, saying he knew just what to do with it. You can image my surprise when I found that crawler under our tree the next Christmas – shiny new, still in its box with its black rubber treads, blade and all! I didn't find out until years later where it came from. At the time, I didn't even consider it coming from The Underground. I just figured Santa made John Deere toys in his shop at the North Pole. I do wish the blade hadn't been removable because I lost it somewhere along the way but I still proudly display that crawler along with my tractor, combine, and grain wagon. I always wished Dad had bought a corn-picker but he always hired someone else to do our picking and baling. I think it was the same neighbor who hired Dad to combine his oats and soybeans.

Anyhow, the shop was in the basement. There was no air conditioning but knowledge now tells me that the earth alongside the building helped keep the temperature inside the shop bearable in the summer when the big doors could be open. I have to think winter was worse. There wasn't a stove in the basement, I guess because of the danger of flame igniting gasoline fumes as tractors were being worked on. Looking back, I find that odd because I remember watching welding being done. I remember, too, giant rubber hoses that ran through openings in the doors to channel out the carbon monoxide. Even without a sign at the back and the doors closed, there was no mistaking the brand of tractors being worked on inside. The "pop, pop, pop" of those two-cylinder engines left no doubt.

The building did not have a furnace. At the back of the parts store was a giant stove that burned fuel oil and had just one heat blower. The stove was just like the one in our dining room at home that heated the entire house but this one was much larger. I forgot to mention that Paul and Ann lived in the apartment above the store on the second floor. I was never up there but I remember seeing a large heat grate in the store ceiling. I am guessing that they either did not have a stove up there or that they used the heat that rose from the store, up through that grate, to heat the apartment. As far as I know, there was only one stairway to the apartment. I remember seeing Ann enter the store through the side door and walk up the stairs behind the parts counter carrying armloads of groceries from Taylor's A & P with one or both of Eric's daughters in tow. I craved the smell of the oil and gasoline that wafted up from The Underground. But I had another reason to hang out there. Laurie Petersen was my first crush. I think we were seven.

The Swedes did little advertising. They bought ads in the town paper, the high school yearbook, and the county fair program. John Deere and Company ran ads in <u>Farm Journal</u> and <u>Successful Farming</u>. Once in a while, there would be short spots on WHOM, the local radio station. ('you heard that from WHOM?' was a common phrase among listeners,). Mel and Del Chalmers, who ran the town's only appliance store, were yet to sell many TV sets in the early fifties. They were expensive and TV reception in Minley was poor at best. That was on a *good* day. People joked that Minley got enough snow in the winter that there was no need to pay good money to see it on a screen in their living rooms.

The big push for Paul and Eric was the annual John Deere Day. John Deere Day was always in the early fall, after the second cutting of hay had been hauled in and either stacked outside or put in the barn, and before it was time to pick corn or combine soybeans. For us farm kids, John Deere Day was one of our favorite holidays, running only behind Christmas and the Fourth of July. John Deere Day and Halloween were a really close contest for third place.

John Deere Day was Paul and Eric's best opportunity, other than the county fair, to showcase Deere's newest line of tractors and equipment. They hoped, of course, to sell new corn-pickers and combines just in time for harvest, but were equally eager to sell plows, disks, and planters for spring. For our dads, it was a day away from the farm between morning and evening chores – a time to socialize with neighbors, see the new equipment, and perhaps to drop in briefly at Ronnie Rivers' Westside Tap. For us farm kids it meant an excused absence from school. Even the kids whose dads used Farmall or Massey Harris machinery went, Paul and Eric hoping to convince the dads to change their loyalties. Even better, it meant free all-you-could-eat hot dogs and soda pops. More than one of us missed school the next day as a result of over-indulging. And it wasn't only we boys who went. Many of our sisters were as avid of "little farmers" as we were.

One of the highlights of John Deere Day took place at the Strand Theater. Dads, some Moms and sisters, and we boys would file into the theater at precisely 10:00 a.m. We would each grab a bag of popcorn courtesy of Paul and Eric and find our seats. I always liked the balcony best. Just like with the regular movies, the show would begin with a *Tom and Jerry* or *Bugs Bunny* cartoon. Next, the screen would fill with black and white images (everyone knew the John Deere colors so black and white was OK) of farmers demonstrating the latest soil and water conservation techniques, all the while showing off the newest equipment. A narrator off-screen provided running commentary as he explained each product's improved features. The John Deere movie would then be followed by a half-hour farm safety story, always with John Deere products prominently featured. Only after all this was done, were we treated to a B-western or gangster movie featuring no farm equipment.

One year, my friends and I understood that a famous Hollywood celebrity was going to attend. He did "attend" but we were sorely disappointed when he appeared only on-screen after the cartoon to introduce the equipment show.

After the show, we kids would head off to the park for free hot dogs and Cokes while Big Swede, Little Swede, and their salesman, Jake, cajoled our dads, trying to sell a tractor, a picker, or a plow. I don't know what killed it but the summer of 1962 came and went without a John Deere Day. Halloween took over third place, uncontested.

A Morning with Del

Melvin and Delbert Chalmers were brothers. In fact, they
were twins – not identical, but twins just the same. They
made no special effort to dress alike but, since navy blue
trousers, white dress shirts open at the neck, and 1950's
crew cuts looked pretty much the same, it always appeared
that way. Once in a while, when the seasons changed and
one would shift to long or short sleeves before the other,
the differences became more obvious.

In my senior year at Minley High School, I took a
journalism class. As a class project, each of us was
assigned to interview a local businessman and then prepare
an article to be featured in the town newspaper. I chose
"Del".

Mr. Chalmers, how did you and your brother decided to get
into the appliance business?

That's a good starter question, son. Minley got its first
electric power plant in 1916 and its first electric street
lights in 1917. People were supposed to begin getting
electricity in their homes that year but the "Great War" put
that on hold so it didn't finally happen until the spring of
1920, a year and a half after the war ended. Homes began
to get electricity, but a lot of folks thought it would be a
passing fad and so many of them held off buying the new
electric "gadgets" offered in the Sears Roebuck and
Montgomery Ward mail order catalogs. Guess they didn't
want to buy something that needed electricity then not be
able to use it if electricity went out of style. By 1922, most
folks had figured out that electricity was here to stay and
the "gadgets" started to become necessities. All of a
sudden, everyone wanted them. It was then that Mel and I
discovered our calling. We opened our appliance store in

the old buggy and wagon factory behind where our store is now. Five years later, I married Alice Petersen. Her brother, "Big Swede", started his John Deere dealership at about that time. People joked that the John Deere dealer's sister was now "Alice Chalmers".

Were you or your brother ever in the army?

Mel and I were born on a farm just south of town in 1902. That made us too young to serve in World War I. By the time World War II came along, we were too old to be eligible for the draft. We both tried to enlist anyhow but neither of us could pass the physical exam.

I had always seen Del wear his glasses with their "Coke-bottle" thick lenses but figured he only needed them as he got older. He pointed to them.

I've needed these ever since the fourth grade. Without 'em, I'm blind as a bat – can't begin to read the newspaper. Mel was born missing the pinky-toe on his left foot. You may not have noticed but it causes him to walk with a little leftward tilt. He says that, if he tries to walk three miles in a straight line, he always ends up right where he started. That's why he never ran away from home or got lost as a kid. Says that's why he's always stayed in Minley – couldn't leave if he wanted.

My dad said Mel was the Great Scorer.

The great what?

The great Scorer.

Well, for about thirty years, he **did** *keep the score book at all of the Minley High School home basketball games – loved doing it. I suppose he did a good job but I never recall anyone calling him* **great***.*

My dad did. Do you remember that sign that they hung on the wall of the gym? The one up near the stage where the scorer's table was?

*"***When the Great Scorer comes to write against your name, he writes not that you won or lost but how you played the game.***" That was a quote by the famous sports writer, Grantland Rice.*

Yes, that one. Dad and I were at a game. He went to nearly all of them when I was little and took me along to a lot of them. Anyway, when I was six or seven, just about old enough to read, I asked him who the great scorer was. He never hesitated, just pointed up to the table and said, "Mel Chalmers."

Smart man, your dad.

Did you ever meet anyone famous?

Well, let me think. I didn't really "meet" him but I saw FDR up close.

Where was that?

Right here in Minley, down where the depot used to be. It was the summer of 1936 and he was going all over the country by train trying to get re-elected. His train made a stop here to take on coal and water. The trains all still ran on steam in those days, you know. So, while the train was stopped here anyhow, he came out on the rear platform. Of

*course, it didn't take long for the whole town to gather even
though most of the residents were Republicans in those
days. He was quite the figure. Even though he had polio
and used a wheel chair much of the time, he had leg braces
and he stood there for nearly half an hour waving and
smiling and talking to use like he'd known us forever. I
think, by the time he left, he'd actually convinced more than
a few of us to vote Democrat.*

What was the funniest thing you ever saw happen in
Minley?

*You wouldn't remember Ed Huckey. I think he was gone
before your time. I'm sure Old Ed didn't think it was near
as funny as the rest of us did but even he enjoyed laughing
about it later. Actually, none of us saw it except the guys at
the West Side Garage, but the whole town heard about it.
Ed, you need to understand, loved to fish. He loved it so
much he even had a second car just to take fishing. That's
kind of common now but it wasn't in Ed's day. Anyhow,
Agnes, his wife, wouldn't allow him to use their regular
car. So, since Ed was only going to use that car to go
fishing, he built himself a shallow tank in the trunk. It
didn't hold a lot of water – enough to keep fish alive maybe
overnight. Had a lid on it to keep the water from splashing
but had holes in the lid for air sort of like a bait bucket
does.*

*It was sometime around the middle of July. I don't
remember the year, but that doesn't matter. Ed had spent
the better part of the day fishing out a Forkney's Pond east
of town. That was the thing about Ed. He didn't seem to
mind the heat. Now me, if it's above about 85 degrees, I'm
not out there. If I'm not working, I'm sitting on my front
porch at home in the shade slugging down iced tea or*

lemonade. But Old Ed, he was a diehard. In winter, he'd be out there fishin' in his little ice shack.

So anyway, Ed, he'd been out there fishin' all day in the heat. He knew how to cool down too. After he figured he got his limit that day, he came back into town an' stopped in at Ronnie's Westside Tap to knock down a couple of cold Falstaffs. When he came back out, that old Buick wouldn't start so he called the West Side Garage and had it towed and walked home.

Well, Ed forgot all about the Buick. The next day, bein' Sunday, he'd promised Agnes that they'd drive to Sioux City to see her sister, Darlene. So, they got up early Sunday, packed up their picnic lunch, hopped into the Oldsmobile and headed out. When they got to Sioux City, it turned out that Agnes and Darlene's other sister was also in town from Denver. So, Agnes talked Ed into staying a few extra days so they could have a nice visit. They all got on so well, that Ed forgot all about the Buick and the fish sitting in the parking lot at the West Side Garage. Well, Jack and Jake, of course, didn't know about the fish but they weren't in a big hurry to get to the Buick so they just let it sit. Temperature went up to about 105 degrees and that old Buick just sat parked there in the sun.

After a couple days, Jake and Jack decided it was time to work on Ed's Buick. It was supposed to rain overnight so they decided they'd get ahead of the game. They hooked the Buick up to their tow truck and pulled it into the garage so they could start working on it first thing in the morning. You've probably got the rest figured out but I don't like to leave anything unfinished so I'll go ahead and tell you the rest of it anyhow. There wasn't air conditioning in those days so, of course, the shop didn't cool down overnight and it stayed sticky humid. Anyway, they pulled the Buick into

113

the garage, parked it next to the mayor's new Chrysler convertible sitting there with the top down and left for the night.

Promptly at 6:30 the next morning Jake and Jack opened the garage. By 7:00, everyone in town knew. Everyone, that is, except for Ed and Agnes who were blissfully eating their breakfast in Sioux City. The mayor came running to the shop to check on his Chrysler but wouldn't go in. Jake opened the large shop doors and put on an electric fan to blow the smell out but that did little good. It only served to thin out the crowd that had gathered to see what was going on. The shop stayed closed all day as Jake and Jack tried to figure out how to get the smell out of both their shop and the Chrysler's upholstery. The overnight rain that was forecast hadn't come and the air was just as hot and moist as they day before. In spite of that, most local merchants opened their stores for business but kept their doors closed.

The news didn't stay just in Minley. The following day, the newspaper in Fort Dodge ran an article headlined **Something Fishy going on in Minley.** *The radio station in the next county wrongly announced that Jake and Jack's West Side Garage in Minley was going to host a fish fry on the town square on Friday evening. Back home, someone overnight posted a sign on the front window of the garage* **Jake and Jack's West Side Garage and Fish Market – Fresh Catch Every Week.** *Someone even posted a sign on Ed and Agnes front porch* **Ed, Take Up a New Hobby!**

How long did it take for it to all die down?

Well, the mayor sent his car to Fort Dodge to get it all cleaned up. The rain the next day pretty much settled the odor. Stores soon opened back up and went about business as usual. You could still smell dead fish in the garage for

114

about a week. Ed came home and bought a half-page ad in the newspaper apologizing to the town. Within two weeks the whole thing was pretty much forgotten except for the ribbing that poor Ed continued to get. He did indeed ditch the Buick and took up woodworking. But for years after there was a saying in town "Oops I forgot to take care of that. I guess I pulled a **Huckey***!"*

What is the greatest excitement you ever recall in Minley?

Good question. That's a hard one. Two really stand out. One was the day the bank got robbed. That was quite a thing but I think the 'great water tower caper' was more exciting.

What was the great water tower caper?

You don't know? I figured everyone in Minley knew about the great water tower caper. It was the night of the big Fourth of July picnic in the summer of 1940. Oh, it was a big deal. The picnic was in the evening that year. The folks putting it on decided that it was too hot to have it during the day. Besides, they figured the farmers could get in a decent day's work and still be able to come and enjoy the evening. So late afternoon, the Lion's Club brought all of the picnic tables from the fair grounds and set them up in the park. Families all brought their own potato salad and hot dogs and what have you and staked out spots. The high school band got set up on the bandstand for a concert. The ladies from St. Elizabeth's had a booth selling lemonade and ice tea and the volunteer fire department sold homemade ice-cream to raise money for new equipment.

Anyhow, the Barnes family had moved to Minley from some big city, Chicago I think but I'm not sure, just before the Fourth of July the year before. The Barnes brothers, Earl

and Lester, said later at their trial, they thought the
fireworks that Minley put on didn't amount to much and
thought everyone deserved better.

Trial?

Well, not really a trial with a jury and all but they had to
have a hearing before the justice of the peace. This is the
way they explained it. You couldn't legally buy fireworks in
Iowa but they had a plan. It so happened that their cousin
from Chicago was coming for a visit so they wrote to him
and asked to get as many fireworks as he could carry in his
suitcase on the train and bring them along. They said they
were thinking a few bottle rockets, some Roman candles
and a batch of plain old firecrackers. I don't know if they
called them that then but he arrived with about five dozen
or so what you now call cherry bombs. They said they were
kind of disappointed 'cause you couldn't really do much
with cherry bombs except make some noise. They were
hoping for something showy.

So, what did they do?

They claimed it was their cousin's idea. For a week or so
before the Fourth they began collecting empty soup and
vegetable cans from everyone who had some. Told folks
they wanted them for target practice with their new BB
guns. Of course, people would have just thrown their cans
in the trash otherwise so they were more than happy to
oblige.

Anyhow, the night before the Fourth, the three of them
climbed up the water tower with bags containing the cherry
bombs and all of the cans. They lined up all of the cherry
bombs around the catwalk that's there for maintenance and
painting and such. They tied all of the fuses together kind of

116

like a string of firecrackers and then set an empty can upside down over each of the cherry bombs. Then they tied a fuse partway down the ladder. Of course, when someone looked up at the water tower from the ground they couldn't see the cans or the fuse so no one knew anything was amiss.

So, the night of the Fourth, the whole community turned out with their hot dogs and their potato salad, drank tea and lemonade, ate their ice-cream, listened to the band concert and waited for it to get dark enough for the fireworks display that the Chamber of Commerce was sponsoring. Meanwhile, Joe Barnes had climbed up the ladder on the water tower. The ladder was on the backside away from the park so no one noticed him. Just as it was about dark enough for the official fireworks display, but not quite yet, he lit the fuse and climbed down.

What next?

Well, the band had just finished playing "The Star-Spangled Banner" and the first cherry bomb went off. Everyone thought it was the start of the show and there was cheering and clapping and whooping and hollering. Then the next one went off and the one after that and the air started filling up with soup cans. Those soup cans started falling into the park and, all of a sudden, the panic started and people began running for cover. Mothers grabbed their children. Folks started diving under the picnic tables. One of the ladies from the lemonade stand tried to duck under the table but knocked it over, drenching her fellow volunteers with lemonade and tea. The fire volunteers sensed that something wasn't right and abandoned the ice-cream to make a mad dash for the fire station. The band abandoned their instruments and joined the crowd heading for the park's only shelter house.

117

Then more cans began falling. Some, we found out later, landed pretty much intact while others had been torn apart by the blast that launched them and fell to earth as shrapnel. And the panic was enhanced by really poor timing. The Germans had just invaded the Low Countries and were marching into France. The Battle of Britain was going on in full force. Everett Hedley, the town's oldest veteran who, only hours before had been the grand marshal of the parade, began shouting and yelling that those "Damned Germans" were bombing Minley! When it was over, Minley's maintenance supervisor climbed the tower to inspect the damage and announced that the tower had sprung a massive leak.

A week later, the Barnes boys were found hiding in the next county over. The spent the next two summers mowing the city park whenever it needed and picking up trash. They also had to paint the outside of the City Hall.

Our meeting drew to a close. I thanked Del for his time and his stories and headed out.

Come back sometime, son. I have more stories.

Bernie Stern

His given name was Bernard – Bernard Stern - everyone in
Minley knew him as just "Bernie." Bernie was anything but
stern, except when his work demanded it. Bernie always
had a clean joke and it was always a new one. No one in
town could remember him telling them the same joke
twice. Bernie always had a smile. Bernie knew how to have
fun. He was always up for a good prank as long as it was
harmless and no one got hurt. Above all, no one should get
hurt. "There's been too much hurt in the world already," he
would say. "No one needs more."

Bernie's amiable nature always seemed curious to people,
given his profession. First of all, Bernie was Minley's only
funeral director and ran the town's only funeral home. By
the time he made his own last trip to the cemetery, Bernie
had buried countless of his friends and fellow businessmen.
He buried Homer Hayward and Clarence Small. He buried
all four of my grandparents, two great-uncles, a great aunt,
and one uncle. Bernie buried Grandpa Ernie, who had been
born a slave but became the unofficial grandpa to most of
Minley's children.

But it was much more than Bernie's profession that made
his laughing and smiling countenance seem curious. It was
his *story.* He was the way he was *because* of it, he
explained, not in *spite* of it. When telling his story to
someone for the first time, Bernie would always begin the
same way. He would roll up his sleeve and show them the
number tattooed on his arm. Then he would explain why he
always smiled.

I heard Bernie's story for the first time the summer I turned
seventeen. We were sitting on Grandpa Ernie's bench in the

119

park, each with a can of grape soda. Grandpa Ernie, by the way, always loved grape soda. And he always told anyone old enough to remember that it wasn't *his* bench. "I'm just borrowing it for a little while." But people, even now, refer to it as "Ernie's bench." "I hope, when I'm gone, that people will come and sit on this bench. Maybe they will think of me when they sit here. Wouldn't that be something?"

Anyhow, I had never seen Bernie's tattoo. He always wore the same long-sleeved, white cotton dress shirt with the sleeves all the way down and buttoned. This he did, even on the hottest, stickiest of summer days. He never appeared to sweat and the shirts always looked freshly laundered and pressed. He could have worn the same shirt at the funeral home, but with a suit coat and necktie. It was the same with his charcoal-grey trousers, his suspenders, and his newly polished black winged-tip shoes. He always wore a hat.

Bernie set his can of grape soda down on the bench between us and rolled up his sleeve. "I'm Jewish, you know."

Everyone in town, of course, knew that Bernie was Jewish. They also knew that his office at the funeral home contained, not only menorah's and copies of the Torah, but also Bibles (both Catholic and Protestant versions), and also the items needed if anyone Muslim should ever require his services. I don't recall that they ever did. There were few Muslims in small Iowa towns during that time. Bernie's neighbors would also see him, every Saturday morning that he didn't have a service to conduct, walk out of his house wearing a suit and a black skull cap and get into his car to drive to the small Synagogue in Fort Dodge. Bernie preferred to walk everywhere on Saturdays and made only two exceptions. Fort Dodge was too far to walk and, if the funeral was on Saturday, he still had to drive the hearse.

He began with his story.

I was born in Belgium in 1919. It was the year after my father returned from fighting the Germans in the First Big War. Our village was a little one, maybe half the size of Minley, maybe smaller than that. It isn't there anymore. Later, you will understand why. Everyone in town was Jewish. Our village was just outside of the Ardennes Forest. Oh, that was such a beautiful forest with its tall pine trees. We loved to take hikes there. And the picnics in the summer! Oh, yes, the summer picnics with Mama and Papa and my brothers and sisters and our cousins. Not far into the forest was a little clearing where we children would go and play fútbol. One year at Passover, Mama and Papa packed everything we needed and we went there and spread a tablecloth on the ground and celebrated the Seder."

I watched him begin to tear up. This was not at all the smiling, laughing Bernie that I had come to know in my growing-up years. I thought about asking him to stop but I didn't. I guess I was curious. I wasn't mature enough to understand that Bernie had gotten through the story many times before. Every once-in-a-while, he just needed the catharsis. Today was one of those days and he had found a listener.

My father taught music and mathematics at our little school and Mama was a seamstress. Ah! Papa loved his music. Every year, they would take us to Brussels or Antwerp. During the day, we would visit the art museums. Sometimes, in the evening, we would go to the symphony or the opera. Papa told us once that, before the war, he loved

121

music by Richard Wagner. After the war, he never performed or listened to German music again.

When I was seven, Papa bought me a clarinet. I loved that clarinet. I played it all the time. In fact, he had to put it away one time for two weeks. I played it so much I was neglecting my studies and failed a geography exam. I had never missed anything so much until then. It was the longest two weeks of my life. I never failed another exam!

When I was seventeen, I went away to Brussels to study at university. I wanted to study only music but Papa, being a very wise man, told me I should became a doctor or a lawyer so I could make a life for myself and my family. Only then, he told me, should I busy myself with music. He said I would enjoy it more if I did it to fill my soul instead of my bank account. Yes, a very wise man, my father. So, I studied biology and chemistry.

In the summer, I always came home and went on picnics in the forest, and played fútbol, and music. In the August of 1939, I went back to Brussels.

*My friends and I had a little study group. We heard stories of what was happening to Jews in Germany. It was disturbing but we weren't in Germany. We were in Brussels, in Belgium. People were coming **to** Belgium to get **out** of Germany. Surely the Germans would not be so foolish as to invade Belgium again after the way the French and the British and the Americans had beaten them in the War. We just never saw the danger. Through the fall and winter and spring, we went to the opera and the museums and parties. We sat at the sidewalk cafes, ate latkes, and drank wine. Britain and France had declared war on Germany back in September but Belgium hadn't. Besides,*

*we knew that if anything were to happen, our larger
neighbors would protect us.*

*On May 10 of 1940, the Germans came. They overran our
little country in a day. I never saw Mama and Papa or my
brothers and sisters or my cousins again.*

I begged him to stop but he insisted on continuing. Several
passers-by saw us sitting on Ernie's bench. They saw the
rolled-up sleeve, knew what was happening, and went on
their way without intruding.

*We – our little group, there were five of us - somehow made
our way to Antwerp, to the docks. There was no point in
trying to go home. We thought that, if we were lucky, we
might still be able to get on a boat to Britain. We got close.
Oh, we got so close!*

*There was shooting going on around us. What was left of
the army was trying to defend the port. We ran as quickly
as we could but got there just in time to see the gangplank
go up. We stood and watched our last hope of escape sail
out into the North Sea.*

*We were among the fortunate ones. We found shelter in the
basement of a Gentile tailor shop. Late at night, his family
would bring us food and drink. He had a button underneath
his counter. Whenever <u>anyone</u> came into the shop, a small
light would come on behind a curtain in our little "home."
As long as the light stayed on, we knew we had to remain
absolutely quiet. When it went out, we could whisper. We
lived there for two years – never saw the sun or the moon
or the stars. We never heard a bird sing. But we heard the
sirens. We were always relieved when we heard them fade
into the distance. One night they didn't fade.*

I looked at his eyes. He was no longer looking at me. He appeared to be gazing past me into a foreign world. I wondered if he was seeing his lost family and friends. I didn't ask.

Only poor Rachael resisted. The rest of us knew that resistance was futile. We begged her to stop, for her own sake, but she wouldn't be persuaded. She kicked. She screamed. But there was no one to hear but the four of us and the SS. She jumped at one of them and tried to claw his face.

He paused. I guessed that he had said as much as he could bear. He pulled out his handkerchief and blew his nose but then continued.

He took his rifle and beat her to death with it, right there in front of us as the others held us back. He looked at us as if he was about to do the same to us. Then he tore off part of her dress and used it to wipe her blood off his gun. He cursed at her for getting it dirty. I remember his words: **"Not worth wasting a bullet!"**

Later, we were loaded onto a train with many others who had also been arrested that night.

We did not know the name of the place where were taken. We later learned that it was Dachau.
We were taken off the train and made to line up along the tracks. The soldiers came along and inspected each of us like a piece of merchandise. The young, the weak, the old, and women with small children in tow were taken out of the line and led away. We never saw them again.

There were large brick buildings. We were told that they were dormitories but we knew they weren't. There were no

*windows. Behind them, in the distance, stood what we were
told were brick kilns. I had never smelled a brick kiln
before but I (we) knew they weren't brick kilns.*

*Every day for three years I pushed a wheelbarrow from the
brick building to the kilns –
back and forth many times.*

He looked down at his shoes.

*I felt guilty with every trip I made with that wheelbarrow. I
also knew that there was nothing I could do. If I refused, I
would be killed and they would simply find someone else to
push the cart. So, I pushed, dumped, and returned to the
big brick building for another load. I vowed that, if I ever
walked out of that place, I would spend my life making sure
that anyone else who ever died, would be buried with
dignity and respect. I promised God that I would never do a
cremation.*

*Finally, the Americans came. We weren't sure what to
make of it at first. Most of us couldn't believe it was
happening. Many of the guards tried to run off but most
were caught. Some were shot. Others were hanged. Those
of us, who had enough strength, cheered.*

*Of our little group, only Avram and I walked out. Actually,
we had to be carried out but then were tended to, fed,
loaded into trucks, and taken to France. I asked to go back
to my village but was told that it was no longer there. What
was left of it after the invasion had been destroyed during
what the Americans called the Battle of the Bulge. Most of
what were now called refugees went to settlement camps to
be housed and cared for until the victorious governments
could figure out what to do us. Avram had family in Cicero,
Illinois. We got to go there. Avram worked in their deli. I*

took a job in a funeral home. I needed to keep the vow that I had made. After a few years, I saw an ad in the newspaper about a funeral home for sale here in Minley. I took the money I had saved and came here.

The previously melancholy face broke into a wide smile.

God has watched over me. And that, son, is why I smile.

I saw Bernie many times after that. I never again saw him sitting on Ernie's bench telling his story, though I'm sure he told it many times over the ensuing years.

After college, I moved away. I came back to Minley occasionally but never ran into to Bernie except at my relatives' funerals. I'm sorry about that now. I should have made it a point to look him up and see how he was doing. Then, one day, I got a call from Dad that Bernie had passed away. I knew I had to come home.

Bernie would have loved his funeral. The whole town turned out – the women in their finest dresses and each wearing a hat. The men all wore their best "Bernie suits" and mostly homemade yarmulkes instead of fedoras. There wasn't room at Bernie's funeral home for all who wanted to come, so his service was held in the city park at the same bandstand where Grandpa Ernie's had been. I walked by his casket and was drawn back to the same feeling I experienced when Ernie passed. Bernie did, indeed, have a slight smile on his face but not the wide one, which we had all come to know. Bernie's best friend in town, who had taken over the business when Bernie's health began to fail, made sure he didn't look stern.

Bernie's service was on a Saturday. Knowing how Bernie felt about driving a car on the Jewish Sabbath, his friend arranged to borrow a horse-drawn hearse from a museum in Cedar Rapids and have it brought to Minley for the occasion. We all walked behind that hearse to the cemetery. A clarinet played a Hebrew hymn in the background as we laid Bernie to rest next to Grandpa Ernie.

Oscar Little

Oscar Little was, at least unofficially, the town pessimist. Fittingly, Oscar was small in stature. He was about Dad's age but, with his prematurely white hair and matching droopy mustache, he looked much older. Piercing blue eyes peered from behind his gold wire-rimmed glasses. He always wore striped Key Imperial overalls when many of his friends had begun to dress in Levi jeans, and either short-sleeve work shirts or plain white tees. While most, by now, wore Timex wristwatches, Oscar tucked an old brass watch in the pocket of his overalls attached to an equally old brass chain. At a time when caps advertising various brands of seed or farm equipment were becoming part of the farmer's "uniform," Oscar was seldom seen without his straw hat and blue bandana.

The scariest thing about Oscar Little was the frequency with which his predictions came, at least in some fashion, true. The earliest such prediction that anyone in town seemed to recall actually coming true occurred before my time.

In October of 1938, Orson Welles had panicked the country with his radio broadcast of "War of the Worlds." A year later World War II had just begun in Europe and everyone was on edge. That October, everyone in Minley was excited and pleased when the owner of the Strand Theater announced that he would be showing "Gone with The Wind" just before Thanksgiving. Everyone, that is, except Oscar. Oscar publicly predicted that, if the theater showed the movie depicting the burning of Atlanta, the Strand itself would burn down.

As I said, this was Oscar's first prediction of such great doom so no one in town gave it more than passing thought.

The first showing came and went without incident. People flocked to see the show and, by the next morning, the great movie was the buzz of Minley. Many who hadn't yet seen it had read Margaret Mitchell's novel so knew how it would turn out. Others who hadn't read it already covered their ears when it was discussed so as not to spoil the ending. By Sunday morning, when Saturday night's showing had also passed without incident, Oscar's prediction was largely forgotten by everyone but Oscar.

The third showing was the Sunday afternoon matinee. Fully confident that nothing would happen, many flocked to see it for a second time. Others rushed to see it before Mr. Findley quit showing it. By the time Rhett Butler's line, "Frankly, my dear, I don't give a damn" shocked the more prudish of viewers, the theater was entirely intact. Even Oscar began to regret that he had missed the show.

Mr. Findley was, of course, pleased that the biggest event in his theater's history had been such as success. Not having had time for Sunday dinner between church and preparations for the afternoon show, he carefully rewound all of the reels and headed home for roast beef, potatoes, and pie. What he failed to do, between the excitement of the day and the anticipation of the evening, was to shut off the popcorn machine. By seven o'clock that evening, the leftover grease in the machine had ignited and the entire building was engulfed in flames. There was little the volunteer fire department could do except to successfully prevent the fire from spreading to neighboring buildings. When the sun came up on Monday morning, it revealed that all that was left of the building was its blackened and ice-covered brick walls. No one blamed Oscar but people began to take him seriously.

Oscar's next prediction occurred during the May of 1940. Mr. Findley had finished rebuilding the Strand in April. To celebrate the grand opening of the rebuilt theater, he had booked "The Wizard of Oz," which had also come out in 1939. He had, of course, been unable to show it. May was the beginning of tornado season in northern Iowa and people in town wondered if Oscar would predict another disaster to strike the town if the movie was shown. Not wanting to either upset folks or deter them from attending the grand opening, Oscar steadfastly refused to comment. One evening though, about two weeks before the showing, he confided privately to his cousin, Orville, that he was very fearful that a tornado would soon strike the town and cause untold damage. Orville proved unable to keep a secret and, within a day, word was all over the community that Oscar was predicting that a great cyclone was imminent.

The Strand showed "The Wizard of Oz" on May 1. Everyone, though a bit fearful, seemed to enjoy the movie and the rest of May passed uneventfully with mild, pleasant weather punctuated by just enough rain to promise a bumper corn crop. Since Oscar's predictions of a crop-killing drought also appeared unfounded, his prognostications of impending doom began to be the butt of jokes and generally regarded as talk by an unredeemable worrywart.

In early June, Oscar predicted that the Germans would soon start dropping bombs on the United States and he feared that Minley itself might become a target. People began regarding Oscar not simply as a worrywart, but some went so far as to call him a nut. The United States was not only in a time of peace, but President Roosevelt was telling everyone that it would *not* be going to war. In addition, Minley, being in Iowa, was far out of the range of any

130

devastation Hitler could deliver. In July, Hitler's Luftwaffe had begun dropping bombs on London and Oscar insisted that his fears had come true. He was wrong, he said, only about the geography. A year and a half later, when the Japanese bombed Pearl Harbor, people remembered Oscar's rantings and, again started to wonder.

And so it went. Through the ensuing years, Oscar would predict a series of both man-made and natural disasters to befall the town and the community. Most did not happen at all. Many others, if they *did* occur, were far less in scope than Oscar predicted. Townspeople generally disregarded Oscar's "doom", calling it unreliable. Even so, though they generally humored him. When they joked about it, it was normally good-natured teasing and Oscar's standard reply was, "Just wait. You'll see."

For some time, Oscar had been eying the aging grain storage elevator on the edge of town. Long past its useful life, the structure had sat empty for over a decade. In this particular year, about 1960 or 1961 as I recall, the oat crop was especially bountiful. Rail cars needed to ship the grain away were in short supply so the feed and grain co-operative decided to temporarily store excess grain in the old elevator until transportation became available. One morning, in mid-July, Minley was rocked by an enormous explosion that could be heard and felt for miles around. Windows were shattered in shops around the town square. Dust and shards of concrete flew hundreds of feet into the air. I was sitting at the soda fountain in Clarence Small's drugstore sipping on a cherry coke, when none other than Oscar Little came running into the store. Straw hat, face, and Key Imperials were covered with grain dust. "The sky is falling!" he was shouting. "The sky is falling!" Indeed, the sky *was* falling. The dust was choking. Pieces of the elevator were raining down onto the town denting cars, shattering windshields and punching holes in roofs.

Did I mention that Oscar owned a chicken farm just south of town? Across the road from the farm, Oscar and his wife, Lula, operated a restaurant called "Chicken Little's."

Minley's Famous Inmate

One of Minley's most famous residents was not a resident for all that long. By the time I would have been old enough to know him, Joe Dove was already serving life without parole at the state penitentiary in Fort Madison. But he was born in Minley and lived there for his first nineteen years, so I guess he counted as a resident.

No one in Minley saw it coming – not Joe's parents and neighbors, not his friends or his teachers. Born in 1929, Joe was too young to serve in World War II. Good looking and popular, he achieved good grades and was captain of the Minley High School football team. In the fall of 1947, Joe headed off to the University Iowa. There was all manner of speculation in Minley about the great success that Joe's future would hold.

I had heard of Dove and, as a child, was fascinated that our little town actually had someone in prison. As I grew older and began to study journalism in high school, I decided it might be interesting to try my hand as an investigative reporter and to try to find out exactly why a seemingly normal kid with such a promising future would end up serving life in prison.

The first stop in my investigative journey was a visit to the offices of the "Minley Weekly Journal."

Minley Weekly Journal
August 2, 1948

Joe Wallace Dove, age 19, of Minley was arrested last Thursday near Fort Dodge. Dove was charged with armed robbery and assault with a deadly weapon after he allegedly participated in the daring daylight holdup of McKesson's Jewelry Store in downtown Fort Dodge. According to police reports, Dove drove to Fort Dodge from Minley on Thursday morning to meet with an accomplice. At approximately 11:00 a.m. the pair walked into the jewelry store and demanded that store clerks hand over cash and an unspecified number of high-value watches and rings. The police also report that, as the two were exiting the store, a security guard attempted to stop them by stepping in front of the door. At this point, Dove allegedly shot 49-year-old Warren Williams, severely wounding him and crippling him for life.

Approximately half an hour later, the pair's car was stopped by Iowa State Patrolmen and the two were taken into custody. Both are currently being held without bond in the Fort Dodge City Jail. It is unclear at this time what prompted the robbery. At this writing, the crime is still under investigation. Dove's parents, Walter and Elaine Dove, have not commented publicly on the crime, saying only that Joe is a good boy and has never before been in trouble.

I learned little from reading subsequent accounts of the trial. Mr. Ferguson, the paper's editor and owner, had gone to Fort Dodge to report on it personally but both the reports and my interview with him produced only eyewitness accounts and procedural material. There was nothing there that helped answer my question about why it had happened. The trial was a short one with five witnesses for the prosecution and two for the defense, one being Elaine Dove. Joe did not take the stand. His only recorded comment was a short apology prior to the sentence being pronounced..

I couldn't interview Joe's parents. Walter and Elaine Dove had moved out of town shortly after the trial and no one seemed to know where they had gone. Someone said he thought they had moved somewhere near Fort Madison to be near Joe on visiting days but he wasn't sure. Joe's former girlfriend had long since married someone else and left town. No one seemed to know where she had gone. None of the adults in town remembered Joe as anything but a bright, talented, clean-cut kid. I called the public defender's office in Fort Dodge but the young attorney who defended him had long ago moved on to bigger pastures, someone said a private practice in Chicago. My resources as a high school reporter in small-town north Iowa didn't reach that far. I was told that lawyer-client privilege would not allow him to talk to me anyhow. The case was growing cold and I began to despair that my stint as an investigative reporter was destined to be both fruitless and brief.

I finished high school and went on to college without giving Joe Dove much further thought. Then, one day, I think it was during my senior year, I ran across an article in the "Des Moines Register" that Joe's accomplice in the crime, Earl Dean Whatley, was shortly to be paroled. My interest in the case sparked back to life and I resolved to resume my investigation. I wrote to Earl Whatley in prison and, to my surprise, he answered back that he would be willing to visit with me after his release. He said that he wanted to come back to Fort Dodge to apologize to the McKesson family, whose store he had robbed, and to seek forgiveness from both them and the security guard whom Joe had shot. He said also that he hoped to live in the community and earn back the respect and trust of his neighbors. Joe, he said, seemed sorry only that he gotten caught and sentenced to prison. The comment regarding Joe's lack of remorse bothered me and I resolved to dig deeper. I vowed, though, not to add to the price that Joe was already paying for his crime by releasing his story during his lifetime.

Soon after graduating college and before starting my first real job, I drove to Fort Dodge and arranged to meet Earl at a small roadside diner just outside of town.

We sat facing each other at a booth near the window. Earl sat staring out the rain-spattered window and then nervously surveyed the diner slowly looking from side to side and front to back. "Habit, I guess," he finally commented as he removed a packet of Camels from his shirt pocket. He tapped the open pack on the back of his left hand until the first cigarette appeared.

"So, how did you come to know Joe Dove?" I asked.

We were roommates in the freshman dorm a University of Iowa.

What was he like? Did he seem like someone who would get into trouble?

He seemed OK, I guess. We got along. We each went to class. Other than sharing a room, we didn't hang out much. You know, man, I'm not the best person to ask about spotting trouble. Trouble has been my life – seemed kind of normal. When I was in high school, I got into some stuff – stuff I'm not proud of now. I was startin' to get it turned though. I promised myself I was gonna be someone. Then . . .

Don't tell me anything you don't want to. I'll listen to whatever you want to share but I've always been curious about Joe.

136

He looked again out into the rain. *He always seemed kind moody. Didn't laugh or joke around much. I didn't think much of it. I figgered' it was just, you know, his way.* He quit talking when the waitress came by to refill our coffee. *Not used to someone doin' that for me. No one poured ******* coffee for me in there. Sorry.*

"It's alright.", I assured him. Dad said it took him a long time when he came home from the war.

Anyhow, he was gettin' ready to go home one weekend and I noticed he'd left his jacket on his bed. I figgered I'd save him some time by chasin' out to the parking lot to give it to him. I was late in the fall 'n it was startin' to get cold. When I picked it up, a syringe fell out of the pocket onto the bed. I put it back I the pocket 'n jus' put the jacket back where it was.

So, you didn't ask him about it when he came back?

*I didn't want to get the **** involved. Sorry again. I figgered it was his problem, not mine. I knew he was doin' somethin' but I didn't want any part of it. As I said, I was getting straightened out. I thought if someone got wind there was that stuff in the room, I get in trouble too – maybe even expelled.*

Did you know what it was?

"Wasn't sure but kind guessed it was morphine. There were lots of guys on campus back from the war. I figgered there were some of them still usin' it for pain or maybe hooked on it. Joe wasn't in the war so I didn't know why he would have it but, like I said, I didn't want any trouble.

Was the morphine why he … you know?

Yeah, that was it. I shoulda' known better. I shoulda'
******* known better. There I did it again. I gotta cut that
out.

That'll come. Go on.

I know, but I'm a Christian now. Either I found Jesus in the
pen or He found me there. I don't know which but that don'
matter. I know He goes there to find people to save. He got
me straight 'n I gotta do better by Him.

I'm sure He understands.

Anyhow, nothing more happened during the year. I guessed
he was still usin' the stuff. I don' know where he was
getting it but, like I said, I figgered it was on campus. I
guess it was from some vet who was usin' it and getting' it
for Joe too.
One night, the summer after freshman year, he called me.
Said he was in Fort Dodge and he needed help 'n could I
meet him. He sounded in a bad way so I agreed to meet. We
met behind a garage that was closed for the night 'n he
begged me to help him. Said I was his only friend in the
world 'n I was the only one who could help him. Man, I
shoulda' jus' called the cops 'n let them get him help. I
shoulda' jus'. . .

Why didn't you?

I panicked. He was in a really bad way. But, like I said, I'd
been in trouble when I was younger 'n I was afraid they'd
think I was part of it 'n haul me in too. I should' jus'
walked away but I couldn' jus' leave him there.

138

So, what happened next?

I told him I'd help him but he had to tell me what was goin' on. He said he'd hurt his back real bad helpin' a neighbor bale hay the summer after his junior year in high school. Said he couldn' let anyone know 'cause he needed to play football so he could get a scholarship at Iowa. Tol' me he found someone jus' home from the war who could get him morphine so he stated usin' it to get him through the summer 'n football season. He still didn' play good enough to get the scholarship but he went to school there anyhow. By then the pain had backed off but he was hooked on the stuff. When he'd go home on break, he'd manage to get a supply.

Go on.

Anyway, he told me his supplier had raised the price 'n he couldn' pay it without getting more money. I figgered he wanted a loan but I tol' him I didn' have money either. He said he had a plan but he needed help. Lord, help me. I was so stupid. He said he'd scoped out a jewelry store that had a lot of high-price watches 'n rings jus' sittin' out on the counter, 'n if he could jus' get some of them, he could trade them for stuff. Said it would be easy. Said he just needed someone to walk into the store with him real casual like, pretendin' to be shoppin' 'n distract the clerks while he sneaked some of the watches 'n stuff into his pockets. I swear I never knew he had a gun. Before I knew it, he was at the counter, pointin' that gun at one of the clerks and takin' watches 'n demandin' cash. Oh, God, I'm so sorry.

Nothing more was said. I thanked Earl, paid for his meal, and told him if there was anything I could ever do for him to let him know. We kept in touch some over the years and still visit now and then but he never asked for anything. He got a job at a feed and grain store near Fort Dodge and has stayed out of trouble ever since. Out of deference to both Joe and Earl, I wrote the story but put it away in a drawer and never published it. Last year, I heard that Joe Dove had died in prison. Earl asked me to publish his story so that others could learn from it.

Mr. Stan

Teddy and I went to kindergarten together in our little country school. Then Teddy moved away and I lost track of him. When we got together again, many years later, Ted told me about Mr. Stan.

His name, Teddy said, was Stanislav Varakovsky. At six or seven years old, I could pronounce neither, so I called him "Mr. Stan" and that was fine for both of us. My parents and our other neighbors simply addressed him as "Stan" and *that* was fine with him too.

Mr. Stan's farm adjoined ours to the north just across a barbed wire fence put there, only to prevent our livestock from straying into each other's fields. At such a young age I wasn't allowed out on the road by myself so, when I wanted to visit Mr. Stan, I would ride my pony through our pasture up to the fence. I would tie Trigger to a post, crawl under the fence, and walk the short distance to Mr. Stan's house.

I'm not sure how old Mr. Stan was when I met him. I'm guessing now that he was in his early or mid-sixties. That would have been early old age back then but seemed really old to me. He would sit there on his front porch facing the road, in his rocking chair, wearing his Osh Kosh B'gosh overalls, and smoking an oversized pipe. Sometimes, he would teach me words from the language people used in the "old country." When many of my classmates in country school were learning to read and write English, I was learning to write and read both English and Russian

With his white hair, mustache, and beard, I could imagine Mr. Stan as Santa Claus if I hadn't known that Santa Claus lived at the North Pole, not next door. Also, I knew Santa Claus to be short and round, not tall and lean like Mr. Stan. Mrs. Stan, on the other hand, could easily have been Mrs. Claus. She was short and plump with white hair and granny glasses that she wore down on her nose, always looking over them. She especially looked like Mrs. Clause when she appeared on the porch with fresh cold lemonade, ice-cream, or a plate of homemade cookies.

I say Mr. Stan was tall but I rarely saw him stand. He had been injured in a farm accident years before and didn't get around well. Also, by the time I knew him, arthritis had attacked his knees forcing him to use a cane when he walked. His son, Georgi, (Americanized to George) had long since taken over most of the farm work. Mr. Stan was able to exercise his two Belgian draft horses though. Like Mr. Stan, the horses had retired but were living out their golden years at the farm. The extent of their work was when Georgi would hitch them up to a mostly empty wagon and Mr. Stan would drive them about the farm or sometimes out on the road. I savored the times I got to ride along.

Anyhow, Mr. Stan and I spent most of our time on that big front porch. He would tell me, in his thick funny-sounding accent, about Russia. I had no idea where Russia was. It really didn't matter. I only knew it from his stories as a magical land covered with snow and ice much of the year and inhabited by strange but nice people and by wolves and bears. I also had no idea why he no longer lived in such a wonderful place. I asked him once but he told me that I was too young to understand. He said he would tell me when I was older. I remember him telling me that he had once been a peasant. I had seen pheasants around our farm and found it impossible to believe that he had once been one but I had always been told not to question my elders, so I didn't. If

142

he wanted to believe he had once been a pheasant, I just decided to let him go on believing that he had once been a pheasant!

Most times, we just sat and talked about things I don't even remember now. I recall, though, that one day I asked him where Russia was.

Oh, Russia is very, very far away.

"How far away?" I asked. "Is it as far away as Omaha?" I had been to Omaha once and it seemed that nothing could be farther away than Omaha. Dad had sent a shipment of cattle on ahead by truck and we followed in the car to the Union Stockyards so he could sell the cattle and pick up his money. I was fascinated by all the big buildings and the busy streets – had never seen anything like it before.

It's way, way farther than Omaha.

I was satisfied that it was farther than Omaha but needed more details. "Did your Mama and Daddy tell you stories when you were little?"

They told me many stories and they told them to my brother and my sisters too.

"I don't have any brothers and sisters," I glumly informed him. "What were their names?

I had two sisters. They were Anastasia and Olga. My brother was Vladimir."

"Those are funny names," I recall telling him.

I suppose so, but not in Russia.

143

"What kind of stories?"

Let's see. There was "The Snow Maiden" and "Little Red Riding Hood."

"Mom tells me "Little Red Riding Hood." She never told me it was a Russian story."

Oh, yes. She maybe doesn't know. And Russia was once ruled by a giant whose name was Peter the Great!

"A real, true-to-life giant?"

A real true-to-life giant.

'Wow!"

In 1954, the United States and Russia were, of course, in the middle of the Cold War. At my tender age, I knew nothing about that. I wasn't old enough to read the papers and we were yet to get a television set. I sometimes overheard the adults talk about the "Soviets" or the "Reds" or the "Communists" but I don't recall hearing anyone talk about the "Russians." All I knew of Russia were Mr. and Mrs. Stan and I loved them.

In the fall of 1956, my bubble burst. It was a crisp afternoon in late October. After school, I had ridden Trigger up to the fence, tied him up, crawled under the fence, and ran to Mr. Stan's porch to tell him about my day. But Mr. Stan wasn't sitting on the porch. I opened the screen door and called to him but he didn't answer. Instead, Mrs. Stan met me at the door. She told me gently that Mr. Stan wasn't feeling well but to come on into the kitchen – that my coming to see him always cheered him up.

144

When I got to the kitchen, Mr. Stan was sitting at the table, hunched over with his head in his hands. I had never known Mr. Stan to cry but I was certain I heard him sobbing. I asked him what was wrong but Mr. Stan, who had never seemed at a loss for words, said nothing. It was then that I saw the "Des Moines Register" spread out before on the table.

RUSSIANS INVADE HUNGARY; HUNDREDS KILLED

Moments went by. I had nothing to say. Finally, Mr. Stan looked up. He must have seen that I was confused. He scooted his chair back from the table and motioned for me to crawl up onto his lap. Mrs. Stan offered me a cookie but, for the first time since I had known her and her delicious cookies, I wasn't hungry. Finally, he spoke. *There are some very bad people in Russia and they have done a very bad thing.*

Weeks, months, and then years went by. I continued my visits with Mr. Stan. Things returned to somewhat normal. We talked, we laughed, and the Russian language lessons continued. By the time I finished the 8th grade, I was nearly as fluent in Russian as in English. Instead of riding Trigger through the pasture, I simply walked up the road to Mr. Stan's porch. In October of 1962, I was just starting high school. Mr. Stan and I had each watched on television the night before as President Kennedy told the country that the Russians were putting nuclear missiles in Cuba. We sat on the porch. By that time, I had begun drinking coffee so we sat and drank some together.

As before, Mr. Stan didn't say much at first but he wasn't sobbing as he had at the kitchen table six years before. He set his coffee on the table between us and lit his pipe. *You're not a boy anymore, Ted. You're a young man. It's time.*

I was born in 1890 in a village about 100 miles east of Moscow. Our village was entirely surrounded by the forest. My father was a carpenter. He would make furniture and sell it to the other people in our village who had cleared small farms out of the forest. They raised potatoes and cabbages and pigs and chickens. We loved our life in our little village and wanted nothing more than what we had. Every year, the Czar's people came to the village to collect taxes. We didn't think it was fair since the Czar hadn't done any of the work but we paid them and didn't complain so they would leave us alone.

One of our neighbors had a grand estate with a large house and much land but he didn't act like a rich man. He sometimes went out and worked his own fields and once in a while came to our village and gave us things. He once paid my father to build a table for him where he said he could sit and write stories. His name was Leo Tolstoy.

Did he ever write a story just for you?

Alas, no. I wish he had. That would have been something. Anyway, in 1914, World War I broke out. You've probably heard some about that in school.

My Grandpa has some books about it. I know America fought in it. Grandma's brother went but he died when I was little so he never told me much about it.

Well, Russia fought in it before America did. I was still a young man and got drafted into the army. They told us we were going to fight the Germans. I wasn't sure why we were supposed to hate the Germans and fight them. I didn't hate the Germans. I had never met any of them so I saw no reason to want to kill them. But I had no say in the matter so I went.

Did you kill any of them?

I'm afraid I killed many. I've always felt bad for them but their leaders had sent them to kill us so we had to do it. But one day, we just quit.

Why?

Well, at first, we were told it was our duty to protect the Czar and our country but we began to have trouble. They started sending us into battle without guns or bullets because there weren't enough to go around. They said to just pick them up from our comrades who were killed or wounded, so we did. People started to say it was the Czar's fault. Then the winter came and we ran out of coats and boots and had to take them from our dead soldiers since they no longer needed them. People said it was the Czar's fault. We lived on potatoes and cabbages. At first, they were plentiful but then there were no more potatoes and cabbages. People said it was the Czar's fault. At the beginning of the war we had meat to eat. Then the beef and pork and chickens ran out. If the Germans killed our horses or if we had to shoot them because they were wounded, we ate the horses. People said the Czar was feasting on fine food while we starved. We believed them. One day, we left our trenches and started walking home. We decided it was no longer worth starving and freezing and waiting to be killed. We figured we would just let the Germans come. We hoped they would feed us.

What happened next?

We started walking home. That's all we really wanted – just to go home. The officers began trying to stop us and some soldiers started shooting them. We were told that, if the officers would leave us alone and if the Czar would step down, we could have a country where the people could be free like in America. But then the communists – we called them Bolsheviks back then – took over and killed the Czar and we were no better off than before. We were still cold and hungry.

What did you do?

Some of us tried fighting the Bolsheviks but they were too strong and there were too many of them. Our group was in Finland. When we finally saw that we couldn't win, a group of us went to Sweden. From there, I came to Minnesota and then to Iowa and met Mrs. Stan and became a farmer.

Leo the Barber

Minley had two barbershops when I was growing up. That seemed to be the case with most small towns. I don't know if that was so each barber could go somewhere to get his own hair cut but that was the way it seemed to be. By the same logic though, the town should have had two dentists and most of the little towns I knew didn't.

Leo Farmer's shop was in the basement underneath Rutgers' Five and Dime. Well, it wasn't a true "Five and Dime" since that name was trademarked but everyone in town still called Rutgers' Variety Store the "Five and Dime" so the name stuck.

Anyhow, as I said, Leo's Barbershop was in the basement. For some reason that nobody ever explained, there was no inside stairway that led from the store down to Leo's. All of Leo's customers had to go into the alley and down an outside flight of stairs. Most of the time, this wasn't a problem. In the winter, it was. If it was icy, not only did the stairs become dangerously slick, but the metal handrail became equally unsafe and unable to prevent falls. For Leo, snow became a source of unequalled dread. There was no room to turn around with a snow shovel in the narrow stairway. The door at the bottom, leading to the shop, opened inward. The screen door, which could have been removed in the winter but wasn't, opened outward, making it vulnerable to snow piled or drifted in the bottom of the stair well. It was thus that Leo had to step down through snow a couple of steps and work facing the alley, throwing the snow upward. Having done so, he would move down a few steps and repeat the procedure. By the time he had worked his way about half-way down, the snow tossed upward would land on the steps he had previously cleared and he would have to scoop the same snow again, tossing it upward toward the alley. And so it went for Leo – the snow at the bottom having been shoveled three or four times before it was finally disposed of.

Leo's shop didn't have great signage. It also didn't have a fancy name like the chain-franchise shops of today. It was simply Leo's Barbershop. And, since everyone in town knew where Leo's was, signage wasn't an issue. There was simply a sign painted on the glass in the corner of Rutgers' window that said "Leo's" with a down-arrow indicating the location of the stairwell. On the side of the building, mounted just high enough on the outside wall to keep a normal-sized man from banging his head, was an illuminated, animated barber pole with its familiar red and white and blue stripes.

Leo's shop had only one window, the one that faced the stairwell. Leo could always tell who his next customer would be as soon as their shoes appeared in the window. Worn, brown lace-up Red Wing work boots – Al Stenson, dairy farmer; always polished black wingtips, grey trousers – John Gray, lawyer, and so on. Leo barely got it wrong unless someone got a new pair of shoes he hadn't seen before. Even then, each customer always seemed to buy the same style he'd always worn. With Dad, it was always black Wellington slip-on work boots.

There were no fancy-dressed singing quartets at Leo's. If those had ever existed as real barbershop quartets, no one in Minley remembered and they would have been long-gone by Leo's time. Neither was there a shelf where each customer kept his own custom mug with his own shaving soap. By the time I came along, Leo had a hot-lather dispensing machine on the mirrored counter behind each chair. What Leo *did* have was a row of green vinyl-clad arm chairs along the wall facing Leo's pair of barber chairs.

There was a radio that always had a baseball or football game on during the season. In addition, there were free-standing ashtrays as well as vending machines for both soda pop and cigarettes. The customer chairs were nearly always full – about half with real customers and half with men who simply stopped in to sit and talk about politics, weather, or whatever was going on around town. I don't recall for sure but I surmise that many jokes were made about wives sitting in the beauty shop across the square spreading gossip.

Leo had two barber chairs but I'm not sure why. To my knowledge, he never had a partner or an employee. The second chair must have been there when he bought the shop. During the time I knew him, Leo gave only two types of cuts. The older generation, such as my grandfather's, favored moderately long hair, always neatly combed and trimmed with the outline over the ears carefully shaved using a straight razor. My dad, his friends, and anyone younger generally sported crew cuts that needed trimmed every two weeks. Butch wax was a staple both at home and at the shop. Dad normally cut my hair at home on Saturday night so it would look nice for church on Sunday. Grandma Gunn normally cut Grandpa's hair with a pair of non-electric clippers and shaved him a couple of times a week with a straight razor. But I often went along when Dad got his crew cut evened up. We always seemed to be in Leo's near lunchtime, when his wife would bring his lunch from home. I think her name was Norma but I didn't know it then. Dad told me later that, when I was small, I would simply announce to Dad, Leo, and whoever else happened to be in the shop, "Here comes Weo's woman."

I don't remember Leo as a young man. He was middle-aged by the time I first knew him. Like Clarence Small, Doc Savage, and most of Minley's other male residents around their age, he had gone to France during World War I. I don't remember him talking much about the war except sometimes when his fellow veterans would occupy the vinyl waiting chairs and start trying to outdo each other with their stories. I *do* remember them all marching together along with the new generation of World War II and Korean War veterans in the community's annual Fourth of July parade. I recall watching the ranks of World War I veterans diminish from both Leo's shop and from the parades. I found out later that, whenever one of his old comrades would pass away, Leo would go to the funeral home and provide a final complimentary haircut and shave so that they would look their best for the viewing.

I also don't remember my last haircut at Leo's. When I used to come home during breaks from college and on later visits, I would go in for a chat and a trim. There was always something about that cut and hot-lather shave that now seems so distant. I don't think the last visit was anything special. I didn't receive any notice when Leo decided to close the shop and retire. So, there was no preparation that this would be my last time. Anyhow, Leo eventually put up the closed sign for the last time and started meeting his friends over coffee at a café instead of at the shop. I remember hearing from Dad in 1983 that Leo had passed away. I hope someone went to the funeral home and gave him a complimentary haircut and shave.

The Travelling Tent Show

The entire town of Minley began to buzz with anticipation each year when shops started displaying window cards advertising Clark Kenyon's Travelling Tent Show. Such shows still drew crowds in those days. Television and movies had largely displaced vaudeville but small midwestern towns continued to crave live slapstick entertainment – at least for a while yet.

The shows were never announced more than a week or ten days in advance in order to avoid competitors from racing into town, setting up their tents, and stealing audiences. The shows were also careful to avoid schedule conflicts with such celebrations as Founders' Day, the County Fair, or Centennials. In Minley, the Strand Theater always tried to avoid showing anything but re-runs of B-movies around the anticipated dates of the show's arrival.

The shows were strikingly similar. Each seemed to feature the same characters but with slightly different scripts and jokes written by the shows' owners and producers. The title characters were always Toby (played by Clark himself), an unrepentant prankster dressed in bib overalls and sporting freckles and a reddish mop wig. His wife, Angela, performed the role of the long-suffering Susie. Each performance would include two or three situation comedies punctuated with acts by magicians, jugglers or acrobats. Some of the jokes and shows, while considered tame today, pushed the limits of so-called family entertainment. Parents could be observed covering their children's eyes and ears or leaving the show entirely with their impressionable, resisting youngsters in tow.

Though I can't say now what year it was, I vividly remember the last time Clark Kenyon brought his show to town and the circumstances surrounding the end of the annual tradition. None of us kids, of course, realized that it was to be was the show's last visit. Suffice it to say, it was not a totally amicable separation.

Clark Kenyon was known for putting on one of the better "Toby and Susie" shows. Though again, the industry standard was not exactly stellar in terms of its dramatic quality and cultural enlightenment. Clark Kenyon, it should be noted, was a first cousin to "Big Swede" Petersen who was Minley's John Deere dealer and four-term mayor.

Though Clark Kenyon steadfastly vouched for the character of his cast and crew and "Big Swede" just as earnestly vouched for Clark Kenyon, the town's residents always eyed their annual visitors with a certain air of suspicion. The night watchman, Minley's only constabulary other than the county sheriff's department, always deputized Al Cousins just for the occasion. Store owners kept an extra watchful eye on both their customers and their merchandise.

The members of the troupe were not allowed to place their tents, travel trailers, or campers in the town square park that comprised the temporary theater. All of the "transients" were, instead, confined to the parking lot at the county fairgrounds a mile or so out of town. Another deputy was assigned to sit at the only unlocked gate leading to and from the fairgrounds to monitor the visitors' comings and goings. There was a list of names and all except Clark and his wife were expected to be back at the fairgrounds at no later than forty-five minutes after the end of the show. Clark didn't like it but the shows in Minley always generated large ticket sales.

154

Large ticket sales meant money so he accepted it despite the grumbling among his employees.

One day in mid-August, it all came to an end. It was the morning before the last scheduled show. Just as the bank was opening for the day, someone wearing a costume similar to Toby's but with a bandana mask over his face, walked in carrying a shotgun. At first the employees assumed it to be a real-life Toby prank meant to publicize the show's finale and that the shotgun was actually a prop gun. They began to laugh and point fingers as "Toby" herded them into the bank's vault. The laughing stopped when he locked the door behind him. He had told them that, if they used the emergency phone to call for help, he would shoot whoever first answered the alarm.

It took "Toby" only moments to rifle the bank's cash drawers. Fortunately, no customers came into the bank. The robber, less the mask and the shotgun, left the bank through the front door and drove out of town in a pick-up truck similar to Clark's.

Within an hour, the town and the roads around were overrun with county sheriff's deputies and Iowa Highway Patrolmen. No one was allowed out of the fairgrounds and search warrants were obtained for all of the campers, trailers, and tents. The entire troupe was gathered in the exhibit hall and interviews were conducted while the searches were going on. That no one knew anything about the heist seemed to law enforcement to be a collective stonewall.

All the while, Clark and Angela were nowhere to be found. The Toby costume was missing from their trailer and the pickup was gone. One member of the troupe confessed to seeing the couple and the truck leave the fairgrounds in the pre-dawn hours while the deputy at the gate admitted to having some beers from his cooler and the dozing off.

All of the other searches turned out to be fruitless. Those assembled were allowed to return to their residences but were warned not to leave the fairgrounds. The normally happy-go-lucky cast and crew collectively decided to boycott the evening's performance. None really wanted to entertain a crowd of people who seemed to regard them as untrustworthy second-class citizens.

As law enforcement swarmed about the town, so did radio and newspaper reporters from Fort Dodge and as far away as Mason City and Sioux City. They seemed intent on interviewing any of Minley's citizens they could snag whether those so-called witnesses knew anything or not.

Around noon, after hearing what had happened, Clark walked into the police station in Boone. It was quickly established that, at the time of the bank heist, he had been having breakfast with the mayor to talk about doing a benefit show for the hospital. They had toured the hospital together and Clark and Angela had then gone to visit Angela's sister.

The fake "Toby" was never caught. There were conflicting stories. One said he was someone local, taking advantage of the town's distrust of the troupe's members. Some speculated that, perhaps, someone from another show had done it to eliminate a competitor. Anyhow, Clark never brought his show to town again. Within a few years, the tent shows disappeared entirely.

Years later, a box mysteriously and anonymously appeared overnight on the front step of Minley's only antique store and consignment shop. The box was labeled "Disguise from the Minley bank heist." Inside the box were a pair of bib overalls, and moppish red wig.

Horst Mueller

Bernie Stern and Horst Mueller would seem to be the most unlikely pair of friends in town. Bernie, a holocaust survivor, was forgiving by nature. He always distinguished between the German people and the Nazis. The Nazis, he explained, were evil incarnate, while the German people had been duped and coerced. The Nazis, he could not forgive. The German people, he could – and did. Horst, on the other hand, had been drafted into the German Army. He loved his native Austria, and despised both the Nazis and Germany. In most other ways, the two of them were more alike than different.

I never heard Horst's story first-hand. I heard pieces of it from other people – Clarence Small, Homer Hayward, my dad, Ronnie Rivers, and more. One didn't ask Horst for his story – one was *chosen.* So, I never asked and was never chosen. Here is Horst's story as I have been able to piece it together.

I was born in 1919, the year after my father returned home from fighting the Americans and the British in France. As was common in that day, I was born at home in our little village near the edge of the forest. I loved the mountains. I loved the forest. There was a little clearing not far into the forest, an acre maybe. We would have picnics there in the summer and play fútbol. In the winter, we would build snow forts and have snowball fights. I would hike in the forest with my snowshoes and fly down the mountain on my skis. I was an excellent skier.

I had a brother, Klaus, who was five years younger than I, and a sister, Gerta, who was seven years younger. My father owned a small meat shop. People in our town bragged that he made the best sausage in all of Austria.

My mother was a cook in a little café and also waited tables and sometimes tended the bar. We had little money but we were happy.

*From when I was very young, I wanted to be an artist. I was always drawing things – trees, lakes, geese, and the little lake near where we lived with the mountains in the background. For my seventh Christmas, Papa bought me a set of paints. I was so happy! "But you mustn't grow up to be an artist," he cautioned me. "Oh no, you must not grow up to be an artist. Your art must be for **you**. You must go to school and then go to university." A very practical man, my father was. "You must become a professor or, perhaps, a doctor or a lawyer. You must learn something that you can feed your family."*

"What about a meat cutter?" I remember asking him.

"No, you must not become a meat cutter either. You must do something more important."

"Then, how about a soldier?" I asked.
*"No!" he told me. "Above all you must **not** become a soldier! Better you should be an artist and starve!"*

When I was ten, Mama and Papa had saved some extra money and took us to Vienna. Oh, that was a fine time. We saw the fountains and the sculptures in the streets, but what I loved most were the art museums! We visited the house where Mozart had lived and went to the concert hall. I liked the music but liked better the music at the beer garden. I never made music myself. I couldn't play and I couldn't sing. When I was in the Christmas pageant at our church,

159

the teacher me to just act like I was singing but not to actually sing. Ha! You would not want to me try to sing now either!

I had two best friends when I was a child. We attended school together and, when we weren't in school or doing our chores, we would play together – often in the forest. They were brother and sister. His name was Jacob and hers was Ruth. I don't recall their last name. It was either Stein or Fein, as I recall. Their father taught music. They were Jewish, of course, and we were Lutherans but that didn't matter. We celebrated Easter and they celebrated Passover. We celebrated Christmas and they looked forward to Hanukkah. In our house was a crucifix, in theirs, a menorah. It made no difference to us.

In the March of 1938, I was eighteen years old. I wouldn't turn nineteen until September. Hitler's army marched into our country. Soon after, it was announced that we were now part of Germany and that we were all to be German citizens, except, of course, for the Jews, the Catholics, the Gypsies, or anyone else they didn't like. There would be no more country of Austria.

There had been rumblings of it for a time that the Germans might come. Some were happy about it – most were not. Fortunately, Jacob and Ruth and their family had already gone to Switzerland and weren't there. They later came to America where Jacob became a lawyer and Ruth became a nurse. I still go to visit them sometimes.
As German citizens, all of us young men were eligible to be drafted into the Wehrmacht. I didn't want to go but, of course, we had no choice. I didn't want to fight for Germany if war came. By now, we had heard stories of what was happening to the Jews and others there. I thought it awful and hoped I wouldn't be forced to be a part of it. I

160

told myself I would rather be in battle and be killed than to take part in such a terrible thing. I hoped I would be captured and sent to a camp in America if Germany were to fight them again. Then, perhaps, when it was done, I could return home and go to university.

This is what Clarence Small related to me as, to the best of his recollection, what Horst had told *him*. He said that something – he couldn't remember what it was – had interrupted them. Horst had never volunteered the rest to him and he had never asked. Later, I told Dad that Clarence had told me part of Horst's story and asked if he knew any more of it.

We were taught how to march. Oh, I hated that goose-step. It felt so ridiculous. Why not just walk? It would have taken so much less energy. But we were told to do it, so we did it. We were taught how to load our rifles and shoot them in the direction of the enemy. We received little other training. We were given uniforms and, when the time came, we went first to Italy and then to North Africa. Our job, we were told, was to protect Field Marshal Rommel's tanks. The Americans and the British, I learned later, used their tanks to clear the field for their infantry. As individual soldiers, we were of no value.

Dad knew little else of Horst's story – said Horst never finished it. He said he wondered if, perhaps, Horst didn't want anyone in town to hear all of it first-hand. Dad, of course, had his own World War II stories but, like Horst, he didn't really like to talk much about the war. I think he shared more with his friends who had been there than he did with me. I knew he was there when MacArthur's army landed in the Philippines. "If you're really curious, you might ask Ronnie Rivers."

"Yes, he told me some of it," Ronnie recalled, "but it's been a long time and he didn't tell much. Said he would later but, to this day, he hasn't said another word about it.

I had studied about the desert in school and seen pictures. A friend of Papa's who stopped by one time had been to the desert in the First War and told me some about it but it didn't seem real. I could not imagine a land without trees or streams or mountains or snow. Even more incredible was that anyone would fight over country like that. Who would even want it?

At first, we were very successful. It seemed that no one could stop us. It was like we had all of that sand to ourselves. Oh, how we cursed that infernal sand! It got into the engines of the trucks, it got into our weapons and our clothing, it got into our hair and even into our lungs and made it hard to breath. We had goggles and put cloths over our mouths and noses but that made us even hotter. My God! The wind and the heat, that awful hot wind!

Rommel's tanks kept advancing but the cost was disastrous for those of us in the infantry. Our job was to go ahead of the tanks and make sure there weren't any land mines. Too many times there were and we saw our comrades blown to bits before our eyes.

By the middle of 1942, we were losing. It was the British and the Americans and the Free French who advanced as we constantly withdrew. Finally, we were trapped and there was nowhere to go but into the sea. Rommel left and went to Europe. Most of the army was captured. We were running out of food and ammunition. We were too tired to fight any longer. I hoped I would finally be captured but our group was put onto a small ship and sailed out into the Mediterranean headed to Italy.

Ronnie was no longer able to help. This was where Horst had left off. "Homer Hayward told me that Horst told him one time about being up on the cliffs at Normandy on D-Day."

"Yes, he talked to me about that one time," Homer began. "I was there, you know. Went ashore at Omaha Beach that first morning."

It was cold. There was a mist blowing in from the channel. The fog was so dense we could barely see past the beach. We heard them before we could see them. There were foghorns and sirens. Soon the shelling started and we knew immediately it was from American and British ships. At first, the shells landed and exploded behind us. But we all knew that they would soon find their range. "Well, they're here," I heard someone in our company say. "This the day we all die."

I was in a rifle company at the top of a dune overlooking the beach. Our orders were that, when the invasion came, we were to stand our ground and fire our rifles until we ran out of ammunition. We were not told what to do after that but I suspected we would already be dead before that happened anyhow. We held our fire. There was nothing to be done yet.

The sun started to come up behind us. The fog began to lift a bit and we could see the ships. "Every ship in the world must be out there in the English Channel." The shells began to land closer. Then we saw the landing craft being loaded with men crawling over the sides of the troop ships. From between our position and the beach, our machine gunners began to open up on the disembarking mass. Still, we didn't fire. We had been told to wait until soldiers

*started coming across the beach and into our range. I felt
sorry for them. Some of the full landing craft exploded
before getting anywhere near the beach. I saw others begin
to unload where the water was still too deep and soldiers
loaded down with equipment simply disappeared into the
sea.*

*Finally, they started coming across the beach and we were
told to fire. My God, it was awful! I couldn't imagine hell
itself being any worse than that open stretch of beach. I
obeyed orders but, all the while, I aimed my rifle purposely
too high, hoping not to kill anyone.*

*When our ammunition ran out, we were ordered to stay in
place. We knew then that we were expected to die there,
fighting hand to hand with our daggers and bayonets.
Meanwhile, the shells from those battleships were landing
closer and closer. I began to hope that I would die before I
had to kill someone face-to-face. I had never done that.*

*By noon, the first Americans reached our position. We had
decided among ourselves that we would not fight. We had
already thrown away our weapons and were sitting on the
ground, hands behind our heads, waiting.*

There's one more thing, Homer went on. You were small.
If you were even there, you wouldn't have noticed it. It was
Armistice Day. That's what we called it before it was
changed to Veterans' Day. The VFW held a ceremony at
the cemetery. Horst was not a member, of course, but he
was there just the same. He stood way back behind the rest
of the crowd. As everyone was leaving, I saw him standing
at the World War II memorial. He just stood there for the
longest time with his head bowed, holding his hat in his
hand. I debated whether to leave him alone with his
thoughts or to speak to him. Finally, I went up to him. He

was still just standing there. Horst spoke first. I could hear his voice quivering. *I'm so sorry. I'm so **very** sorry. Please forgive me.*

"That's all of it I know," Homer went on. "You need to talk to Eric Petersen over at the John Deere Store. He's the one who brought him here, you know."

"Yes, I brought him to Minley. I never got overseas, you see. After basic, I shipped out all the way to Nebraska. I was assigned to a unit guarding prisoners at a POW camp. They were treated well. Most were happy to be there. They were out of the war, well fed, and had barracks, for the most part, as good as our own. There was little trouble, and any that there was ended up being directed at each other rather than at us. The ones we trusted most were loaned out to local farmers whose own sons were still off fighting in the war. They were, by and large, friendly and willing workers and it certainly helped to keep the farms running."

"I was assigned to supervise a group who were helping one of the farmers to haul in his hay. That's where I met Horst. He told me he missed home and wanted to go back when the war was over. I had heard talk that the Russians might take over Austria and so I shared that with him. That was when he asked me if all of the prisoners would have to go home. I told him I didn't know. By then I had told him all about Iowa and said he might like to go there until things "settled down" in Europe. I told him that, if I was still on duty when the war was over and it was time for the prisoners to be released, I would see if I could help him. When that time came, I was able to. Dad offered him a job fixing tractors at his dealership but he declined, saying he wanted to start a meat market. So, Dad loaned him some money and he did just that."

I had first met Horst when I was a small child and Mom would take me into the market. We raised most of our meat at the farm and Horst actually came out when we needed to butcher a hog or a steer. But that sausage! We loved that sausage. Dad asked him once if he would make us a batch with our own pork but Horst, being in the business of *selling* sausage, politely refused. I remember that sausage as a treat, both growing up and when I would come home for holidays after I moved away. By the way, that shop was the best smelling place in all of Minley.

I also learned from Eric that Horst was worried whether or not the town would accept him. Once word got around that he had been drafted, was from Austria- not Germany, that he had never been associated with the death camps or even rounding up the victims, he was readily accepted. In fact, his store was next door to the VFW Hall.

Horst joined the Chamber of Commerce, prayed alongside veterans at the Lutheran Church, and even provided free meat to the VFW for their cookouts and chili suppers. He was an avid booster of all Minley High School sports, bought yearbook ads, and even catered the annual football banquet.

Most of all, Horst became fast friends with Bernie. When they found out how much they had in common in their childhoods, they became nearly inseparable. It was not uncommon to see them sitting alongside each other on "Ernie's bench" in the park. I never asked Bernie if Horst had ever told him his whole life story and, if he did, Bernie never told anyone.

POSTSCRIPT

Horst still lives in Minley. I was there a couple of weeks ago visiting my sister. I saw him sitting alone on "Ernie's bench." I took my can of grape soda and approached him. He looked so worn and fragile (he's 96, after all). He was just sitting there staring across the square toward the meat shop. It had long since changed hands but it was still there. I nodded at the empty seat beside him. "May I?"

"I remember you," he told me. "You're Sammy Gunn, aren't you?"

"Yes."

Did I ever tell you about my life? I was born in 1919, the year after my father returned home from fighting the Americans and the British in France . . .

The Minley Baseball Club

The Minley Baseball Club never practiced, never played a single game – never even took the field. They had neither uniforms nor gloves. Didn't need them. What the team *did* have was a team captain, Clarence Small. Clarence was chosen unanimously by the club since he had once met the great Ty Cobb and had an autographed bat and ball to prove it.

The club had caps. They weren't called baseball caps – they were mostly seed company hats, same style, different logos. Some bore the insignias of "John Deere" or "International Harvester" but most were ones handed out by feed and seed company salesmen selling products such as "DeKalb", "Pioneer," or "Moorman." Clarence, since he was the only one in the group who wasn't a farmer, wore one advertising the "Pittsburgh Paints" that he sold in his store.

The Minley Baseball Club never had rain-outs. Instead, they had sun-outs. They *did* have a schedule – of sorts. Each Saturday afternoon during the season, whenever the weather wasn't fit to work in the fields, they would meet at Mel and Del's Appliance Store. When all were present who seemed to be coming that day, they would line up and trek up the stairs to a loft overlooking the sales floor.

The "clubhouse" was filled with discarded furniture that the team's wives no longer allowed in their homes – a saggy dusty sofa with springs sticking out so that sitting down was an adventure, a recliner that no longer reclined, and various other pieces generally unfit for human "habitation." Alcohol was neither served nor allowed at the games though TV announcers Dizzy Dean and Pee Wee Reese constantly extolled the virtues of Falstaff Beer. Elwood and the "Old Pro" did the same with their cartoon antics during commercials. The sole libations came from a pop machine that stood downstairs behind the washing machine display. Popcorn, peanuts, and chips, however, were abundant.

The Minley Baseball Club had no "local" team to root for. The Minnesota Twins were still the Washington Senators and would be for several more years. There was one televised game per week that generally featured the New York Yankees, the New York Giants, or the Brooklyn Dodgers playing each other or the Cubs, the White Sox, or the St. Louis Cardinals. The Athletics were in Kansas City but hardly ever made the airwaves. The lack of a local team did nothing to diminish the team members' fervor. There were rabid Yankees fans and Red Sox fans who were equally fanatical. And there were favorite players. What partially fueled the fanaticism was that most well-known players appeared for the same team season after season. There was hardly a thought of the Yankees trading Whitey Ford to Boston or the Red Sox dealing away Ted Williams. It just didn't happen much.

The club's TV set was black and white, and so small as to be nearly invisible from more than a few feet away. Again, it did matter. The club was able to see the game. What mattered more was when the picture was so snowy as to be barely recognizable or the "vertical roll" caused the picture to constantly and rapidly move to either the top or bottom of the screen. Sometimes either Mel or Del were able to help by adjusting the set or going to the roof and adjusting the antenna. More often, the only recourse was the radio. If the game itself happened to get rained out, the team would simply set up a table and play cards.

And so, it went - season after season. The team eventually disbanded as more and more of the members got TV sets at home. It's said that the ghosts of the team's members still gather in the loft and that one can sometimes hear the whispers of once-loud boos and cheers. It's not the "Field of Dreams," it's just what Mel Chalmers fondly called "The upper deck."

A Country Doc

If ever there was a doctor whose last name didn't fit, that doctor was Hal Savage. No one ever called him doctor, as I remember, or even Hal. It was always just Doc.
Doc maintained his office conveniently upstairs over Clarence Small's Rexall Drug Store.

I never met Doc as a young man. By the time I was old enough to remember him, both his hair and mustache had turned snow white. He had developed the slower gait that comes with age and a pronounced stoop that I always assumed was from spending so much of his life hunched over bedsides.

I'm not sure how old Doc was when I first knew him. It was said later that he had delivered probably half of the people living in the community. That half included both of my parents, most of my aunts and uncles, nearly all of my cousins, my siblings, and myself.

Doc had to be nearly the last of his kind. When virtually all other doctors had given up making house calls because their time was too valuable to spend traveling about the countryside, Doc still did it. Monday, Wednesday and Friday, he would see patients in his office. Tuesday and Thursday, he would crawl behind the wheel of that old blue Hudson to drive the town's streets or stir up dust along the county's back roads. Mabel Green's rheumatism made it painful to leave her chair and she had never driven a car so she had to rely on neighbors to drive her to town. Doc would drop by. Clyde Brown's breathing difficulty made it hard to get up and walk the few blocks uptown. Doc would drop by with a stethoscope and a smile.

Doc's nurse, Thelma Barnhouse, was a different story. To us kids anyhow. It was always a relief if she didn't come along when he visited. Nurse Thelma was much younger than Doc, closer to my parents' age. Her first job out of nursing school had been with a MASH unit during the Korean War. The boys old enough to know what the term meant called her "The Drill Sergeant," but never to her face. Others called her "The Marine" though she had actually served in the army.

Doc had the gentlest touch that I have ever felt from a physician. He had a way of making a tetanus shot feel little more than a tickle. He would say before the shot, "This will only hurt a little," and actually made it come true. Thelma could say the same thing and then stab you in the butt with a bayonet. Thelma was fairly new out of the army and had only been working with Doc when she came to all of the country schools to dispense the newly developed polio vaccine.

We began to feel queasy the moment we saw that mint-green Chevy pull into the drive at the edge of the school yard. When time came for the shots, we were all assembled in the school's only classroom – nine grades of us, fourteen kids. One by one the teacher led us around the corner into the little room that served as the kindergarten room. Our apprehension grew as we watched our schoolmates led off into that room and then heard the ominous shrieks and crying that followed.

For some reason, Thelma started with the youngest and worked her way up to the two eighth grade boys, Rich and Ralph Jackson. The younger kids, after they had been "shot," normally got a bit of sympathy. By the time Thelma reached the fifth graders, the sympathy was all used up. It was Rich's turn. Instead of waiting in the kindergarten room, Thelma came out and stood in front of the schoolroom near the chalkboard. "Next," she'd call. Rich looked positively white as he rose from his desk near the back of the room and slowly mad his way forward. Drill Sergeant was getting impatient. "Hurry up, young man! I've got three more schools to visit today."

"Ow!"

By now, Thelma had lost both sympathy and patience. She scowled as she called for Ralph. To our teacher's horror, Thelma apparently had a flashback to her MASH days. "I can't believe you even felt that! You boys are g-damned cowards! When I was in the army, I put needles twice that size in boys' arms and they didn't even flinch! Some only had one arm left to put them in. What a bunch of crybabies you are!"

Fortunately for Nurse Thelma's job security, she must have been good at what she did. She remained as Doc's nurse until after I left for college.

In journalism class in college, one our assignments over Christmas break was to do an interview with the citizen of our hometown whom we most admired. I immediately thought of Doc. Though he had finally retired by then, he was still in amazingly good health for his age.

"Doc, what made you decide to go be a doctor?"

"Well, it was natural, I guess. I never gave much thought to doing anything else. My father was a doctor before me and his father before him. My grandfather actually served as a field surgeon with General Grant's army in the Civil War. I was born in 1888. When I was 10 years old, my father went

to Cuba as an army doctor. I really missed him while he was gone but Mom kept telling me how important his work was. There was yellow fever. They didn't know what caused it back then and Mom was always worried that Pop would catch it from one of his patients and die. Anyhow, he came home and practiced medicine in Sioux City before he moved here to Minley."

"What did you like most about being a Doctor?"

"I liked helping folks get better, of course, but I mostly liked delivering babies. There's just something about bringing a new life into this world that always made me warm inside, even after doing it for so many years. I guess next to that, it had to be helping some go out in peace and comfort after living a long and fulfilling life. Most times, they had smiles on their faces and that gave me comfort too."

"Was there anything you didn't like?"

"That was not being able to help someone – sitting there helpless and watching them slip away when they should have had so many years left and watching their families. Many times, I felt like I had let them down even though I had done everything I knew how to do. Children were always the worst. There's nothing so sad as seeing a mother or father watch their child die. I hated that part. I guess the other thing that was just as horrible was when there was an accident and someone could be alive and healthy and then just suddenly gone. I couldn't sleep at all the night after your Uncle Wilbur had his car wreck.

"Grandma and Grandpa never blamed you."

174

"I know they didn't but, still . . ."

"Was there ever a time you wished you weren't a doctor?"

"That's a pretty interesting question. Not really but, again, there were a couple of times I felt entirely helpless. I felt like, if I weren't a doctor, folks wouldn't expect me to help but, since I was, they expected me to be able to work miracles. One of those times was when I was a young doctor just back from the army in 1919. There was a great influenza epidemic. Someone could waken in the morning as healthy as a horse and be dead by midnight. It was all so sudden. Seemed like there was no time to do anything for them and no one seemed to know how it spread or how to prevent it. The other was the polio epidemic. What a vicious disease! I was a grown man by then but I nearly cried when Dr. Salk proved that his vaccine could actually prevent it.

"You said you served in the army. Are you OK telling me about that?"

"I went to France in the First World War. It never occurred to us that this was World War I. It was the Great War and we all hoped and believed it would the last one ever. How naïve we were! I was a brand-new doctor then - so unready. I had heard my grandfather talk about field surgery during the Civil War and it all seemed nearly as barbaric as battle itself. I wasn't at the front but near enough to hear the noise of the artillery and rifles and machine guns. Then the ambulances would come. I thought I could talk through it but I need a minute. Sorry . . . Anyhow, the ambulances would come and the orderlies would unload the wounded. We had to walk among them and decide which ones we thought we could take into the surgery and possibly save and which ones we couldn't. We

175

felt like we had to play God. I can't tell you how relieved we were when they told us an armistice had been signed and the war was over. I remember when the movies, "Sergeant York" and "A Farewell to Arms" came out. I couldn't even go see them. I had seen too much already. When the Second World War broke out, I cried like a baby!

"Dad said you made house calls with a horse and buggy."

*"Your father exaggerates. I'm not **that** old! Well, I guess there were a few times. I made calls before a lot of the country roads were either paved or graveled. Sometimes, it was too muddy to take my car. Sometimes the snow was too deep. Once in a while someone would come for me on their tractor and take me out to their farm. On occasion, I just rode my horse with my bag slung over the saddle, but that wasn't often. Most times, I actually drove my car. I think the night your Dad was born, I went out to your grandparents' farm in a bobsleigh, but your Dad wouldn't remember that!*

Doc lived to be nearly 100 years old. I think it was 1986, or thereabouts, when I last saw him. It was a warm spring day and we sat together on "Grandpa Ernie's bench" under a shade tree in the town square. Doc was still as sharp as could be. He seemed to remember nearly all of the people he had delivered and treated over his nearly sixty years in practice. He even remembered me. Since many of them had passed by then, doctor-patient privilege no longer applied. He told me things I had never heard about some of the town's most prominent citizens – no one's deepest secrets and nothing salacious or embarrassing – just *things*. He was the town archive. I don't know that he ever wrote any of it down. Someday, I *will*.

Made in the USA
Monee, IL
11 December 2019